Songs for Olympia

Tomoé Hill

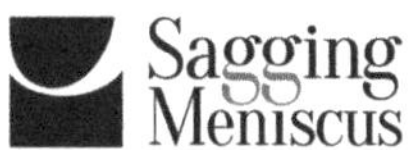

Set in Mrs Eaves with LaTeX.

ISBN: 978-1-952386-67-1 (paperback)
ISBN: 978-1-952386-68-8 (ebook)
Library of Congress Control Number: 2023937215

Sagging Meniscus Press
Montclair, New Jersey
saggingmeniscus.com

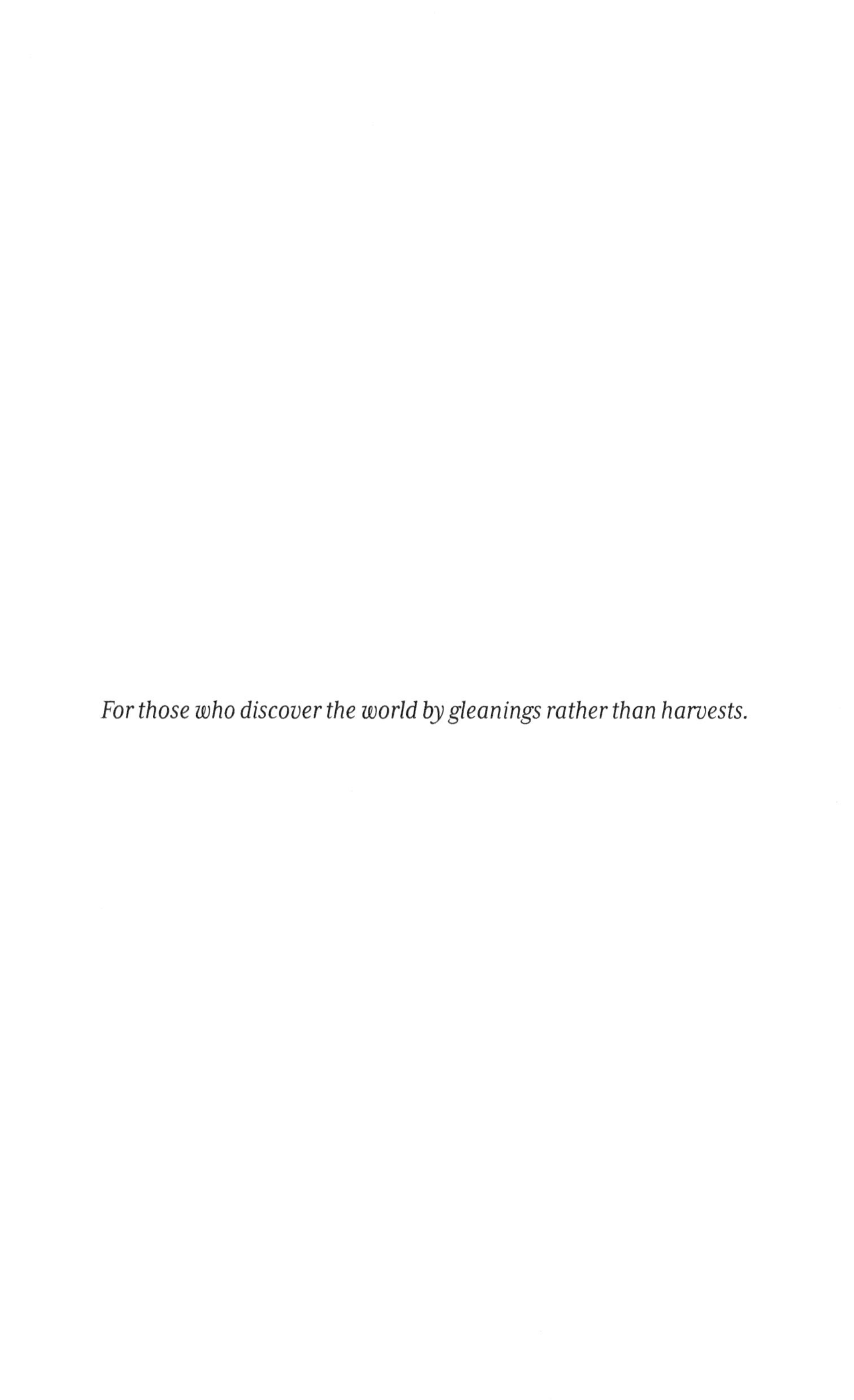

For those who discover the world by gleanings rather than harvests.

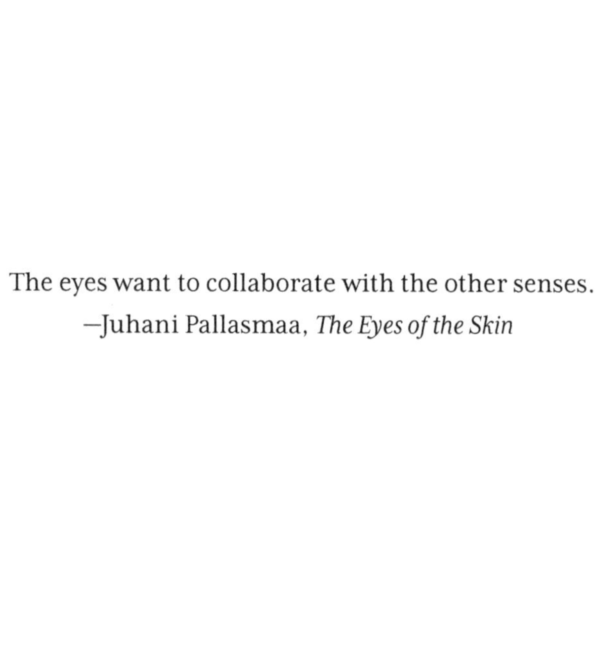

The eyes want to collaborate with the other senses.

—Juhani Pallasmaa, *The Eyes of the Skin*

Foreword

The Ribbon at Olympia's Throat by Michel Leiris (I have based my writing on the Semiotext(e) edition translated by Christine Pichini) is not a book about a painting, despite its title. Leiris, that great chronicler of the internal and introspective external, used Manet's famous and controversial painting as a prompt to explore his reflections and anxieties on writing, illness, age, modernity, and desire—observations from a life which was drawing to its close. His fixation and expansions on Olympia's ribbon in this particular work have been described by Lydia Davis as the 'expressive power of fetishism', while she notes his sentences as 'labyrinthine'; this is key to understanding any Leiris. Whether brief or seemingly endless, they function as Theseus's golden thread, bringing him mind to mind with the Minotaur at its centre, the writer himself. In this case I say *themselves*, for where Leiris has gone I have attempted to follow, unravelling my own red thread along the way. *Songs for Olympia* is a response to a response: an imaginary conversation that finds its commonality in the black circlet whose pull we have both been unable to ignore.

Songs for Olympia

1.

IT WAS SUPPOSED TO STOP but with the fury of something constrained for so long it continued disregarding the body it could not exist without. Not just the once but twice, three, fifteen, forty times until she could no longer count, tired of the days which left her drained both literally and figuratively, gazing pale at an unknown reflection in the mirror. Once she was white over red, new in her mother's arms, now she was red over silver bleeding onto the ever-accelerating world, her body changing again faster and faster while she could do nothing but lie supine, let it escape and consider her detached image blood-framed, fixing her eyes beyond the body, beyond the ages which had sped by in a flushed blur, beyond the judgements of what she was and what she was not, like all women thus framed. She reached up, half-asleep from loss, and felt the line which partially circled her neck; the mark of Olympia.

2.

There is nothing left to shock but everything, in the landscape of her body. 'Unable to tattoo everything he had in his head over the surface of his skin, he decided . . . to confide to paper.' *Now* is an excess of both, Michel, skin and revelation. But what would you make of it? It is a post-coital haze for those who have never had the pleasure of orgasm, a confusion ignorant of its riches, only able to recognise its flaws. You and I seek pleasure in meaning and meaning in our pleasure. Here, where paper is flesh, intimacies are only visible to those who care to read, beneath the warmth of the skin.

3.

The flowers which the maid holds as gently as a newborn are what my eye is first drawn to. The blurred bouquet of pale blue, white, and reddish-pink with accents of greenery. This is Manet slyly declaring Olympia as the new Marianne; sex as liberté, égalité, fraternité . . . sororité! Lost in discerning the blossoms—are they dianthus, anemone, chrysanthemum?—I think of Cy Twombly's flower paintings, then *Venus + Adonis*, with its great amorphous pinks like spent bleeding hearts both anatomical and floral. When Roland Barthes, writing about Twombly, says of other artists' work, 'there are paintings which are excited, possessive, dogmatic; they impose a product, they turn it into a tyrannical fetish', one could say Olympia embodies this—if the gaze is invested in the tired myths of form and subject. But to break the gaze, look with what Barthes again refers to as 'reversing the usual relationship in classical technique' in an otherwise typical genre, one starts to properly see: Olympia, her surroundings, and objects are transmuted. She rejects and disdains: invitations come to nothing, exposures of flesh (and the denial of them) are testament to an agency that dares the viewer to take unique pleasure, rather than the replaceable object of fantasy. Flowers become symbols of freedom, the cat, back arched, would sooner scratch than purr. Even the maid's eyes and gestures are knowing: the bouquet as the old viewer's gaze understands it—the admirer's token—will shortly be resigned to an ash heap. Olympia herself flickers like an illusion: the awareness of sexuality and the determination to make it one's own, a figure passive at first glance, but seething after.

The flowers linger. A single white enormous bloom within the bouquet's centre: carnation or chrysanthemum, pure love or death? At a Japanese restaurant in Paris, the dish set before me of fish and petal fragments. *What is this?* I ask. The woman is unable to find the precise name of what is still fresh and bitter on my tongue. She thinks for a moment. *Cemetery flower*, she finally says, then smiles. The taste of death, sharp as memory. There is no doubt it is a carnation rather than chrysanthemum which demands Olympia's vague attention, sweet and clove-redolent. But would she turn her head with new interest had it been a gift containing a memento mori in exchange for her desirability? Instead of mere love or empty admiration, a consideration of beauty and the inevitable end, whether it be death or time, the latter so often seen as the lamentation of women. I can see Olympia amused, even aroused, plucking each petal and leaf, eating it. If this is all, this life, then I devour both its pleasure and grief; a gesture of true eros. The lover who loves what will wither and perish as much as what blooms offers high adoration indeed.

4.

In responding to your words, Michel, I am responding to myself. Observing Olympia with you, I see us as a tripartite Sibyl: we are the ones, as Heraclitus said, with frenzied mouth(s), but she is the one speaking through us.

> *I'm speaking in order to speak: when I speak, it's certainly to say something, but (speaking frankly) I don't know what.*
>
> *I am on the edge of that madness that treats soliloquy as dialogue—that thinks citizens of other kingdoms—including the kingdom of the unspeakable, which is entirely internal—and language itself could communicate with me through some remarkable stroke of luck.*

I do not speak—outwardly—in order to speak. For all the times the only ear to hear me has been the one in my head, I have thought, is that madness? You and I and how many others, Michel, have said this to ourselves, a silence so great that it seems impossible to think that we could have not have felt this great solidarity as a kind of external, unknown force. I am deliberately talking to some part of myself, that hidden lifelong confidant when there was no other. Now I know I straddle a line between worlds, a stray silent phrase or feeling coming into the view of my consciousness which becomes the start of a conversation, a communication with another kingdom.

> *I want to say. And, that said, I'll say everything that speaks to me. Even if I shout if from the rooftops, there'll be nothing you can say about it.*

I have said everything I want to say, so when my mouth opens, there is a déjà vu clinging to the words which emerge, a spider's web holding fast to its prey. To whom did I say this or that, was it myself or another body, was that body in my head, on a page, or—most unlikely—in front of me, something I am so envious of when I see the ease of it in others? What is this, then, coming out of me? When I write, am I just writing the same things over and over, speaking in tongues: having always known these words, but knowing not what divinity has placed them there?

> *I only speak . . . to quiet those things that leave us speechless, that prove that one day nothing will say anything to us anymore.*

If I am speaking or writing—for they are two different things—in my mind, have I said anything at all? Here is the edge of madness again, where nothing is quiet yet everything is, a mute stream of speech that flows through my head at all hours, opened lips from which nothing comes out. You say we 'expend so many words talking about words' but these are still the days where nothing says anything but we keep repeating it, the meaningless meaning that forms our new Babel. But here, Michel, on the page that lies written and overwritten in our heads, you and I are building a tower not towards God but Olympia.

5.

My mother had a translucent porcelain tea set, hiding and revealing its veins of colour when held up to the window. But the true fineness of such a cup can only be discerned in the dark by touch, when your hands attempt to translate the creation of another. I see the door curtains behind Olympia, their near-closure inviting darkness, and want to shut my eyes as I did as a child, my fingers seeking the patterns and textures of her skin on the page, journeying along the paths of her body as they began to travel along my own.

6.

When I stand there in front of her eggshell skin—despite its form and expectation of its treasure, there is always uncertainty in what lies just beyond—with its black circlet, I think she must look back, wondering why it is we price, prize ourselves so cheaply? She knows it is her emptiness which sets the value because it demands everything, a display of nothing setting desire ablaze with the weightlessness of possibility. I look at my own blank warmth and know its treasure lies in what can be written on it then erased, a dream within a dream. The histories of many, traced in invisible liquids, are the freedoms of pleasure. Jezebel bejewelled, this new virtue, this ribbon, is still worth far above rubies.

7.

Did the model Victorine become Olympia in the way a character like Flaubert's Emma Bovary was furtively claimed by everywoman in her morning mirror? Ordinary Victorine, once realised on canvas, forever after repainted in private fantasies with awkward brushes. We indulge in private surfeits of self-recognition; the secret personas we are and those we wish to be, stretching into infinity. Did she look at herself after and whisper *c'est toi, c'est moi, ce n'est pas moi, je suis les deux*, tilting her head towards a reflection whose murmured response was not unlike the muted rush of a seashell, understood only by her ear?

8.

Serge Lutens Mauve de Swann—that is the colour of Olympia's lips. £58 a tube. I change my mind: perhaps they are Pat McGrath Divine Nude or Venus in Furs (£28, £35). Or Tom Ford Quiver (£44). The more I search the more sex seems inexplicably linked with the dressing of lips, down to the cost—a tithe for ritual adornment. In spite of myself, I find more. Rosebud, Suspicion, Call it a Day. The relentless projection of desire, guilt, innuendo, judgement. I look at her mouth again. Instead of a signalling red inviting others to take a reverie-inducing bite it is a respite to envision them in dream-tinted lilac, the shade of memories belonging only to her, the costliest of them all.

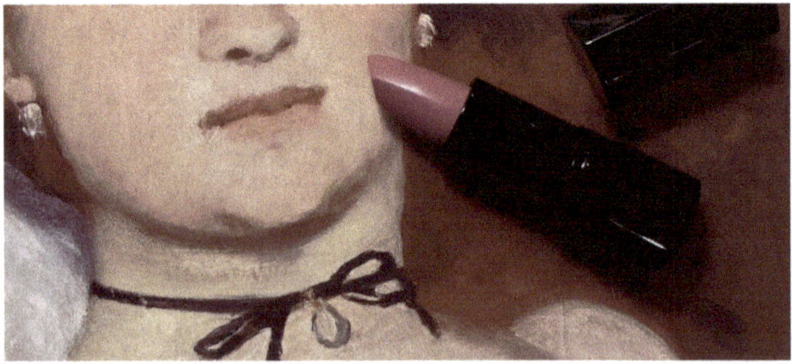

9.

'Or other fragment of a body through which magic may be practiced.'

If the ribbon is the fragment, what is the magic? Yes, Michel, I know it is not *the* body, but the point of the object is to project the body: the ideal, the fetish, the mysticism we both worship and repel, often at the same time. If the body is the vessel, then her ribbon is the drop of water, the darkness which causes the primal to spill and surround us with waves, sweeping us up in its inexhaustible brutal rhythm. But it is only nature, this sort of dance, and being the only creatures or phenomenon in the world without, we must create or at least imagine our own. In a production of Verdi's *Macbeth* I once saw, the night dance of the witches was portrayed as a sensual, sexual fit. Disjointed chorus lines synchronised in their arrhythmia, they rode giant cocks like wild hobbyhorses as their tinnitic heads pointed in all directions. Melodious shrieks rang out and reminded me of the mating calls of the racket of parakeets in our nearby wood. Finally spent, the witches collapsed upon their grotesque members just as the birds' love-withered voices always seemed to float down, subsumed in the forgotten winter's mass of decaying leaves.

10.

I wonder what anxiety it is that renders me unable to fix a shape to my words, the desire for an immaculate form in which I can neatly separate these thoughts and ideas like those ordered wooden drawers of typed cards that I so loved in the library as a child. Here is an idea! And another, and another, but always briskly explanatory in the manner of a doctor presenting a patient with the mysteries of their bodies in the most succinct of terms. I present myself with an executioner's tools, sharp edges to guillotine thoughts which ramble like the ivy reaching and holding fast to every conceivable surface ('it's as if plants were growing out of your chest'), but the moment my mind turns to what comes next I can feel its tendrils alert, searching for another grasping point. Perhaps as a result of this, in the garden I have let the canopy of ivy and grape consume the very light it needs, and in return it occasionally sheds its excess leaves and blossom as a reminder that I belong to them; instead of cursing its riot, I am seduced by their tart, bittergreen scents and the audacity of their appetite for occupation, the greed for survival. I know that like the garden, I should just give myself up to these growths and paths, the desire to place a cord of greenery around my neck and become not just bound but possessed, their ever-shifting forms like Twombly's pinks and my own blood which insist on presenting me with Rorschach blots, chess pieces: *what do you see? What do you see?* I see everything in all directions, all perspectives, trying to cling to a world which has never clung to me.

11.

To be held like an insect, perfectly arranged in the amber of sexual scandal, is to be part of an era all women have known. Ambre, anbar, *caution*.

12.

The neck seems a pretense; a distraction which suggests erogenous interest placed at a distance to its centres—both actual and symbolic—is higher-minded. The ribbon as a declaration of delineation, the animal varnished, even vanquished, with civility. The other day I came across a 1984 advertisement for Boucheron jewellery: a close-up of a woman's breast, small but perfectly formed like Olympia's, her pinkish-brown nipple aroused and wreathed in an elaborate necklace of diamonds, rock crystal, and emeralds. The breast celebrated, victorious, and ornamented, a statement which could be nothing other than what it was. Olympia! A new reign heralding the glory of sex in its pronounced specificity, her queen's kingdom and the ever-yielding bounty of her flesh. Framed in jewels, an exclamation of the body which refuses all chaste contemplations.

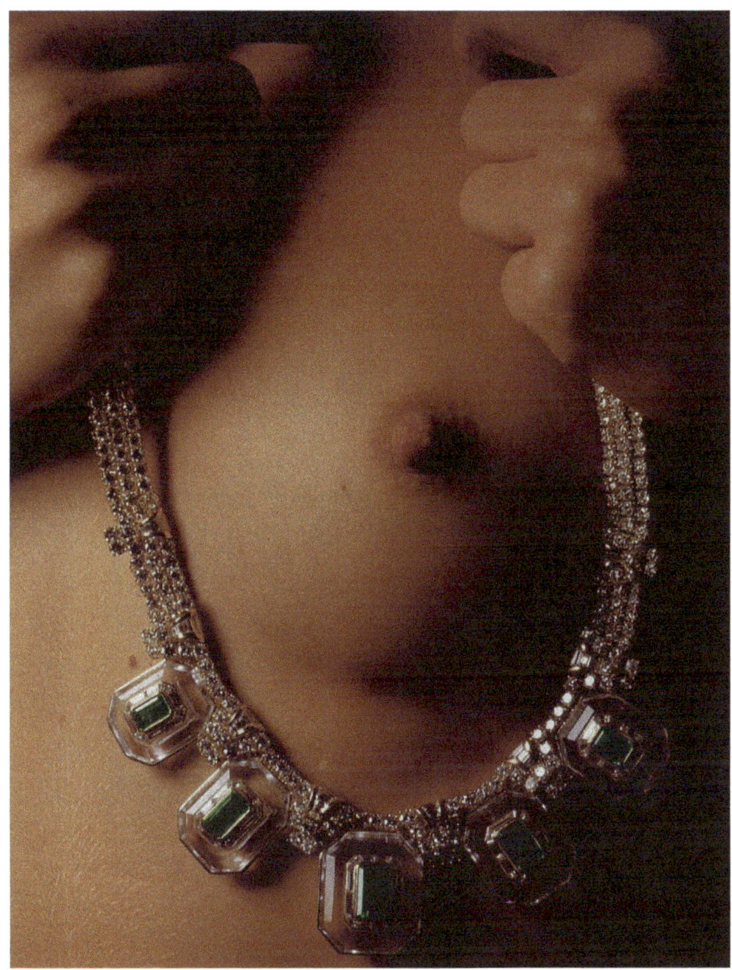

13.

If we do not learn from history, Michel, neither do we learn from fantasy. 'COURTESAN REALITIES STOP . . . YEARNING FOR REALITIES GIRLS TO TALK TO AND MAKE LOVE'. How amusing it is to be able to pluck your imaginary counterpart from literature so easily, in this case Maupassant's Georges from *Bel-Ami*: 'he was waiting, too for something different, less vulgar, a different kind of kiss'. Why is it, real or not, you wish to transform courtesans into ladies and ladies into whores? Chasteness tinged with indecency as if it were a seasoning, vulgarity always with a touch of innocence, for it is always you—Michel, Georges, and the rest, on or off the page—who wish to be our saviours, teachers, creators. And yet, like Georges, who cannot admit he owes his own transformation to women, what I see in Olympia is a woman who in her unreal form holds a mirror to you, in which you only see yourself.

14.

There is something about Olympia's flesh-tint, barely tinged with blood, which recalls syncope, that drop of pressure which causes fainting. It is not reminiscent of weakness, but the strength of rising again, a resurrection as powerful as a morning glory in repeating bloom. The sensation of such change is literally dizzying, but also hand in hand with a strange excitement. Her first experience of it was during a weekend life-drawing class: straddling a wooden sketching bench, she felt strange and removed. Thinking she was merely nauseous, her gait that of seasickness, she walked to the bathroom as evenly as possible. In the empty white ceramic-tiled room she looked in a mirror watching blood drain from her face, a chameleon adapting to their surroundings. A hand raised revealed the same, the undertones of hue disappearing, the green-blue veins in greater contrast. Her mother's teacups, held to the light. For a few long moments, she felt there would be a transformation; from flesh to charcoal, alabaster, or paint. In the reflection, the start of a waxen glow that when gone too far can never resume its flush, resulting in final stillness. It is an odd beauty, still more odd to watch such a change in oneself, not thinking of the reality of such a state, but the romantic paths instead. This is a fancy of youth which cannot grasp an end of self. At the lowest ebb of pressure, her eyes started to close as she propped her hands against the cool glazed white of the tiles, cheek against the glass; half in one world, half in another. Orphée clinging to the mirror, wishing for entry. In those few blank moments she was an unfinished drawing, a half-filled painting, a statue's skin, unblemished by excess noise and colour of life. But as the slow rise of blood inevitably returned, with it came an invincibility, a renewal that must be physiological and the also the mind's relief at coming so close to an unknown. We explain the world by what we observe: the deep violet-blue morning glories covering a wall of the grey garage, closing every night and unfurling every day; a loss and a rush in a girl's body on the cusp of womanhood and its echo in a woman's when it resumes its slow closure; Olympia, perennial.

15.

Until now, I had not remembered for years when I was very small, my mother had worked part-time for a florist named Bev, whom I called Grandma Krueger. Bev was a slightly tough, good-natured older woman with a voice like Johnny Carson, prone to laughter. I only ever saw her dressed for work in a dark-blue smock, headscarf to tie back her thick grey hair, and glasses on a chain so that she could take them on or off depending on whether she was creating arrangements or serving customers. To me there were two worlds of flora: of sun-warm gardens or woods, and the cold ozonic scent of the refrigerated cases of her shop which I would associate with buying eggs, margarine, or ready-bake biscuits all sharing the same scent of suburban homogeneity. Tall narrow black buckets of red roses, carnations, lilies, ferns. Lying on her fluorescent-lit worktable, green foam blocks damp with a special preservation mixture, an enormous roller of wrapping paper, thick metal shears, twine. The cased flowers seemed alien counterparts to their garden siblings, never aging and forever multiplying. Though I knew my mother worked in other flowers, like gardenias set to float in bowls of water, it was the others I understood as a particular language: roses and carnations for love, lilies for religion and death. Set in these contexts, one knew the messages of their deliveries. Regardless, Bev was always cheerful, whistling as she built wreaths destined for funeral homes or laid long-stemmed roses in white-papered boxes for lovers. White and red became synonymous with life and death and love in my child's mind. One day Bev came to the house with a present for me, a tall doll set on a stand, a blonde-haired, wide-eyed woman in a splendid red velveteen hooded dress trimmed with white fake fur and holly berries. It was the berries that bewitched me, having a mirror sheen like that of ripe cherries and when pressed, slightly soft to the touch—it seemed perfectly natural Bev should give me something adorned with its natural opposite, like her chilled blooms. I resisted for months, until some strange longing burst and one day I sank my teeth into them, breaking through the thin coating into hard white foam smelling of nothing; as satisfying as eating the mulberries I would gather from trees when out walking with my father. It is not that I ever doubted, Michel. 'The detail we touch with our fingers, bait we sink our teeth into' is a question of desire where the torment is not one of disbelief but that of wanting to become.

16.

If anything, Olympia is a constant reminder that I have been frozen in time for any number of people who crossed my path at one point or another in my life and no longer are anything but footnotes; the natural act of any collector of emotions. Very few of us remain active memories in others, still breathing, engaging, with those selves inside of us not quite folded away in tissues in the attic of our consciousness. But those active versions of ourselves living in someone else's mind are as out of our hands as Victorine was when Olympia existed for the greater world; used like marionettes attached to their wooden frames and strings according to the inner conversations of our past relationships or acquaintances, speaking words we do not recognise or else ones we do, infinitely repeating. I think of those framed versions of myself every so often, first surprised that I would exist in such a private gallery, then curious at what those versions of me look and sound like: am I classical statue or figure, or an abstraction of feeling in primary colours? Am I a soundscape or a soundless video of a looped moment, or am I forever captured as short brutal words howling against the starkest of backgrounds, the essence of what was left once I was gone? My own inner gallery of lost persons are not works of art as such, but scents: kept under bell jars, that I might lift each one and immerse myself in their olfactory cacophonies, a cloud of invisible perfumes reanimating into flesh and blood, limb and muscle. They need not speak so long as I can continue to breathe them in and touch; sensory mementos more true to our voices than voice itself.

17.

'Modernity, eternity' redux: screens full of an infinite numbers of Olympias, a moveable feast providing a surfeit of choice for the fantasy-gorged multitudes. In her mind, she plots a life separate from the infamy of her images. Turning weary from the bed or couch on which she poses, away from the screen to pull on clothes which allow her a moment's blessed anonymity from the camera eye of desire.

I struggle with the idea that we could ever achieve a real modernity in the way we are told is possible, Michel, because to be truly modern suggests we need have no dependence on the past, something continuously suggested to us in utopian commerciality. If it is a constant cry now that such modernity has eroded us as whatever the idealistic essence of to be human is, then I only have to remember the Olympias of now, and know modernity is simply a vision that chooses to forget what it has previously seen, as if what the eye takes in creates a world which renders us free of the past. I think of the idea of modernity in my own past, and realise then we lived outside of it necessarily, not being able to afford the accoutrements of a new world—in that sense, I could be said to have never been modern. To say these things are more accessible now is correct for many, but it still denies modernity because the ideal of such a state is play, and most are left clinging to these toys as a lifeboat of relevancy: the necessity of living, the need for simple acknowledgement. But the speed of modernity does not look back, nor do one's playmates. It becomes the most obtuse of choices, to step out of modernity even to the smallest degree. To do so is rejection: of people, of ways of life. It is dropping back when you run with others and accepting the empty space around you. But I am used to this, Michel. Well-acquainted with those spaces first from illness then lack of money, that emptiness represents something new, in the way a small garden offers possibility which a vast crop does not. The yield of a crop has immediate purpose and a destination, while the fruits of the garden may never come to be, but are equally as likely to flourish in a way that its forced occupation of a particular space and tending expects of it. I am used to my empty spaces and knowing that what comes from them hold more value to me, in writing, in people, in attempting to form a life. And if I am not modern, then likewise, these Olympias are not, and the original Olympia would likely find herself in understanding with her sisters now. The modern eye is still the eye which sees her for what she is not, then moves on to the next, one Olympia becoming three, then nine, then eighty-one, then six thousand five hundred and sixty-one . . . the same unmodern woman trapped in a modernity in which she has no agency. And it is easy enough to delude oneself that with this eye upon you, briefly, you too, are now modern. Then you feel the speed of it rushing past again and remember outside of this world you must create your own present, a platform in which to securely rest and view in order to understand where it is you have come from and where you are going. And this is why I love Olympia and her sisters, for I understand the eye and the speed which we can never hope to be a part of, the brief relevancy which never actually sees us beyond its own aims to consume the new and move on. Unraptured, we can go back to the empty spaces which belong to us alone, tending to the women we are. In this solitary world the eye and mind linger: over the verdigris of the savoured words and images left to the chance of time, over bodies whose flesh reveals their own stories, indelible but visible only to us. This parallel present is a respite from the rapidity of the other world where we exist only as a static moment, little more than a hiss in the system whose restless sibilance becomes more deafening by the day.

18.

But you spoke of music and writing and modernity, the awareness of the first discovery of something else; without being able to articulate, the feeling that sets itself apart from all the others which starts to create one's personal discernment of the world. For me, e.e. cummings was that first awareness, though I knew 'modernity' no more than 'eternity' bar the latter as the unspelled word of freedom in a fairy tale. On encountering his poetry, it felt as if we were long-intimate though unfamiliar companions, despite looking on the page as if a child was assembling letters in a way that was instinctually pleasing. The poems did not speak to me, but instead chattered with me as well as to themselves, content in their brokenness as if they were a wise child or an adult suspended in ideal simplicity. I had a perfect understanding of his incompletions, silences, and abstractions, parenthetical asides and punctuation marks that articulated themselves more than the other complete sentences I had read or heard. He had learned to communicate in the way children stop and start, translating the directness of emotion into an innate shorthand. Later, when I discovered Sappho, she as well seemed to be another out-of-time example, as if both were unearthed by a forgetful age turning out its pockets. You say '*eternity* . . . gives the resounding sensation of being other than in the temporal' but I think eternity still adheres to time, where Sappho and cummings have always felt dreamlike, a memory and a voice that moves from body to body like a sibyl, possessing. Have they always been there, or is it that their ephemerality exists beyond time in the ether of understanding, only making themselves known to us when they deem us ready to receive their messages?

19.

I am too harsh about you, Michel. In honesty, my criticisms of you are the same ones I whisper about myself, and if I damn you in one moment for appearing to see only one version of yourself, I must confess in the next it is not true, that your complexities are mine; we are both plants rooted in the same pungent earth of sex and death and memory. Is there a difference between your gaze and mine, our lust towards and fantasies of Olympia? As Marguerite Duras says, 'the thing that's between us is fascination, and the fascination resides in our being alike.' I know that in poring over this painting, it is my attempt to find another kind of depth, one which sets me apart from you—profundity as ascension; in ravishing Olympia, to become raptured. But there is nothing to be saved in all this thought. One must understand that to feel unrelenting pavement beneath the feet, gaze upon this strange

Eden on canvas recognises both the innocence of wanting to be beyond knowledge and the luxuriance of carnality. You hold fast to the ribbon at her throat to keep you true while I clutch at the invisible one about my own, wondering what truths tighten around it so.

20.

The end of the world (or at least the nth attempt at it): mass displacement, partisan finger-pointing, armchair experts, the scramble to justify dirty money, empty supermarket shelves, indifference, detachment, anxiety, amusement, horror, silence, dead airwaves, everything doctored except the wounded, low phone batteries, war NFTs, guilt for trying to be normal, guilt at a lack of performativity, guilt for trying to write about a painting of a naked woman in the middle of death (as well as the inevitable guilt when I'm not, for as you say, 'regret when I do bad work, regret when I don't work at all.'), guilt for sleeping, guilt for not sleeping. We have all lived under war of some kind, or have lived with its consequences and tangents, myriad and ensnaring as any spider's web. War is a possessor that is never possessed, though its cleverness lies in *yours*, *mine*, *theirs*; the hierarchy of suffering which turns backs and closes doors. Creating of delineations of justification in such an entity only ever ensures it will consume all as easily as it would one, without the prejudice we have projected upon it ourselves. I am the granddaughter of an Army doctor, seeing men go off to WWII, and the distant relation of someone who had fought in the Japanese army, so disturbed by what he had been part of that he afterwards withdrew from the world, the daughter of a mother born in the aftermath of unspeakable violence in a country who had attacked the country she came to live in decades later, the child of parents who met in Israel at the time of the Six-Day War. Atrocity has small beginnings; there are many who would ignore them as unrelated inconveniences. War goes from unseen to overlooked, bloated by the bodies that made it fat, and we stare, its vastness incomprehensible. I have lived with the remainders and reminders of this ignorance and gluttony because there is no such thing as moving on. It is less than some but more than others, and I know there is nothing you can do but live according to what life accords you. Such mythic experiences are only taken as truth by others whose bones have been gnawed by the same beast. In the poem 'Forms of Forts' by Susan Stewart, she writes:

> *You cannot know both hands at once;*
> you must choose between the living and the dead.

Yet the shadow of what was forever obscures the light of what could be. Guilt is a memory of the lives which cannot be led at the same time.

21.

Having read your pages of regrets with sympathy—knowing full well I dare not attempt anything similar beyond a brief allusion to regret or anxiety—I came to the end of your litany, face to face with 'who knows too well that "I" is not *an other*'. Despite realising that I might have misunderstood your meaning, I found myself filling with the familiar rage which I have spent a lifetime unsuccessfully pushing away, only able to see the sentence in a particular context. Have I been *I* more than *other* in this life so far? When you spend so long in small battle proving your *I* does not necessarily bear the weight of every other *I*, that it wishes to stand alone, there are moments when exhausted, you let go and let the tide of assumptions wash over you, thinking *today is the day I let myself drown*. You take in the water and gag until some unbearable reflex forces you to push your head above again and make your way to shore. This happens not once or twice, but so often that you cannot imagine life without it. Let me tell you a naïve story, Michel.

When I started writing, not so long ago, I needed to break away from a 'we' that I had let myself become subsumed by, what felt and still feels like a shameful desire for proof not of ability as much as completion, independent of others. I wrote terribly and alone, then slowly not quite so terribly, but still alone. Motivated first by a rage—the need to prove that *I* was worth its solitude—it dissipated, leaving only the words, and the work of words; and as you know full well, even a lifetime of that work still leaves one dissatisfied with its results, so it was not often I was satisfied. Our materials do not judge—like Olympia, it is the audience which does more cruelly than even ourselves, cruelly because whether fantasy or reality, the eye of judgement can never quite see with the eye of the creator and all we can do is bear it in silence. I thought for a brief time that my *I* could rest here, free to move back and forth between two halves of a person. And it was, for a time, true. Suddenly, I found myself pulled apart: one half desired, the other shunned, the words not as important as whatever my *I* was being claimed for—two others, depending on who read me. Was I supposed to be grateful when I saw the announcements loudly exclaiming my importance, that *I* (the exotic other) was needed? A lifetime spent fighting reduced to red lanterns, cherry blossoms, exclamation marks, the word *truth* dangled like a rancid carrot to me, whom they assumed were starved—as if this was the validation of my scars I had been waiting for, to simply follow whoever it was that bellowed the hog call of identity or scattered crumbs of recognition. And recognition bestowed not to me, but them, as if I had not spent a lifetime making a silent truth for myself from the scraps left by people once finished creating the dolls of my perceived image, content with being left alone because it meant no interference. Would it erase the echoes of *Jap* by children unaware of what they said; the deliberate mangling of my name; the exaggerated scrutiny of my face; the corners of their lids pulled high as they laughed; women who regarded me with suspicion and men who equated exoticism with promiscuity? What a casual liberation it is which is bestowed by people unconscious of what it means to live with a weight you will eventually also be buried with, no matter what small peace you might find. Whatever temporary sanctuary this blank page, was no longer. I would not choose one half of myself over another, any more than I would disdain the half which is derided as problematic—do these would-be liberators think I have lived hating a part of myself instead of questioning why it is people were so afraid of something so unassuming? In some ways, it was easier to be ignored by all, free to examine both halves of myself without the unbearable pressure of having to purify myself in the eyes of others' virtue by choosing a non-existent better half. I have refused to do anything asked of me. You learn to function on a diet of numbness and dismissal, the only way to navigate a world's fixation on the other—whichever other that is. *I* was simply *I* in all the complexities that no one cared to notice, and if there was no question of its normality within my own family, then I would attempt to proceed likewise through the world, stubbornly oblivious. Now, this strange celebration makes me feel as if I were witnessing my own funeral: where does one go after the *other* is of no use, its ashes undetectable as the dirt it now rests in? For it is a particular *usefulness* which is the focus: My use is as the animal in the zoo, the show of exoticism, the *other* writer in its artificial habitat—kept well, but still caged. Skin serves a purpose, but the lesson some of us learn is that ours serves another's: do we go along with it in order to more easily get what we want, or turn our backs on it completely in order to preserve who we believe we really are? Elspeth H. Brown, writing about the Asian American mid-60s model Kedakai Lipton in *Work! A Queer History of Modeling*, says that while Lipton felt assimilated and accepted to a degree, there was no doubt she remained scattered across a cultural spectrum that saw her as both enough and not enough in terms of representation and identity. Now it feels like whatever little sense of sameness we had which transcended a cynical targeting of identity is gone forever. A sense that to make clear one's particular social, sexual, and cultural identity differences must necessarily take precedence over any shared humanity lest one be seen as an identity traitor or indifferent to social justice. To be seen—arguably the primary currency of our time—requires one to both call attention to those differences and militantly emphasise them, rather than be lost to the unthinkable invisibility of privacy: trying to find some personal contentment and fulfilment in the world. If you ask me to define what I am, all I know is whatever it is—indefinable as it is—can never meet your expectations, and therefore we remain forever separate, an identity between us which neither recognises, because one's life can never fit the imaginary skin created by the other. So what is left but to walk away, run away, keep both halves silent, only show myself in glimpses here the way I always have, knowing to reveal anything in a larger manner is to not be read but only displayed? Sometimes *no* must be taken up as an identity: the deliberate choice to obscure in a glaring world, to guard in order to know and possess oneself. We know the saying about the road to Hell, and I am familiar enough with that path to not be moved by its new decorations. I have no regrets or anxieties, Michel, just that familiar exhausting doggedness of old: not knowing where it is I go, I continue to move ever forward, towards a utopia as inaccessible as eternity.

22.

If I speak of Olympia, then I speak about women, and so I must ask myself why, having had few female friendships. Maybe it is the case that I look at her duality, even multiplicities, asking questions of myself, attempting to discern my non-place in a world of women. And in writing I am aware it is never complete: of my own blood, I have written of my mother and not my sister, to whom I do not speak. The absurdity of it is, every time I try to write her, I imagine pushing her back into the womb. Not out of jealousy but an attempt at rebirth, a game where we take turns recreating ourselves in the hope we will finally recognise each other as kindred unequals. My poor mother, who gave birth to two halves of a daughter which resisted any attempt at coming together, poles forever in repulsion.

23.

Sitting at the kitchen table in the evening, her mother would teach both her and her sister to play Memory with a pack of her father's playing cards, Piatnik 'Tudor Rose', thick and glossy with detailed illustrations of various English personages: Queen Anne, Marlborough, Richard Lionheart, Anne Boleyn, the card backs patterned in green, red, and gold with the namesake rose in the centre. She would shuffle with the surprising skill of someone intimately familiar with a pack and lay them face down on the second-hand wooden table. Including the yellow-clad jokers scattering their gold coins in jovial warning—for the children demanded it—she would have them take turns choosing a card, trying to guess where its match was, their little hands hovering over the identical patterns as if they provided a second pair of eyes. Luck and sight—what a strange partnership opportunity and observation are, where the turn of a card or spin of a roulette wheel is no different than the turn of a head, one marking while another is marked. Is this the moment where she learned to unconsciously seek a connection for everything in the world, the gambler's obsession the same as that of child's? What she knew from those evenings was that possibility was everywhere, to be seized by those whose eyes and intuition are wide open to it.

24.

It was some years before I saw my mother at rest. Even when she sat at the kitchen table, playing cards with us or reading, she was never truly restful; they were only pauses between the endless labours of motherhood. I have no memories of her being sick, or even in bed, though this must not be true: she appeared to me perpetually standing, walking, or in some other sort of motion. I must have been on the cusp of my teens when I found her sleeping on the sofa one day, apparently so exhausted by her near-miraculous energy that she was forced into an unnatural horizontal position. Her skin was waxen and bloodless-pale, drawn tight around the temples and jaw, her left arm slack over the edge. What I witnessed did not appear as rest, instead resembling the pose of the *Pietà* (consuming such artistic imagery as a child, almost every scene or emotion you come across has its matching reference), restless death rather than respite, but I was, for some moments, watching and listening to her almost imperceptible breathing unsure if there was to be a resurrection. After what seemed a while but was only a long minute, her eyes opened and she sat up, little colour returning before she smiled and continued with her tasks as if she had never known that temporary break from verticality. For that stopped heartbeat of a minute I glimpsed her as she was, not as the world saw, the fragility of a person whose every image and action was the result of her projected representation—mother and wife—instead of whoever it was she had been before us and continued to be beneath the perpetual exterior of her constancy.

25.

She rarely kept photographs. A small handful was what remained of a life meticulously categorised by her parents, a story she would do her utmost to disassemble. *Why*, she asked herself. After so many years, the answer was the same: that face within the borders of thick Polaroid or Kodak photo paper, a shifting reminder that the subject never sees itself as the object—of desire, familial love, or the particular narrative of the one capturing the story—and likewise, the object can never quite relay its secret stories to the one who has so carefully organised their life in images. She was always at least two people and perhaps more, this multiplicity of selves unreconciled leaving her determined to upset any clean explanation of herself wherever she found them. Sifting through the detritus of images, she realised she had unconsciously created another album in her mind: one of only women and kimonos, a story that looked within and without its paper frames of tradition and modernity, the one of who she was and who these other women were, the true subject which no one chose to see.

The mother once told a story about her wedding day: after the civil ceremony, having had a drink or two but not being a drinker, she thought she was a bird. Flying down the Main Street of a strange city against the blue horizon of a lake with its fish so unlike the ones of her homeland, flapping the wide arms of her flower and crane-adorned cream silk kimono, she thought she was free. The streets and buildings of Sapporo where she came from were an intuition, a memory map whose features felt as warm and alive as the skin of those who inhabited them, a territory of birds which understand place from presence alone. Even though she now finds herself in a city chaotic with numbers, where both houses and people are numbered in multiple forms, her first knowledge is through a kind of flight and touch. Forever after, she will know these streets by the wingspan of her silk sleeves, the tapping of her lacquered zori on the even cement.

In a downtown photographer's studio, she wears the kimono again, her black hair pulled back in a splendid bun held in place with a long ebony and coral pin. Kneeling on the floor against a pale backdrop, she places her hands on her newborn daughter, both slightly open-mouthed with captured laughter. Wrapped in a red-patterned kimono of her own, she waves her hidden arms like a fledgling nesting in padded cotton. Gaston Bachelard, writing about nests in *The Poetics of Space*, says the images we attribute to love come from 'a dream of protection' akin to armour or shelter. 'Dreams of a garment-house are not unfamiliar to those who indulge in the imaginary exercise of the function of inhabiting.' As soon as she can recall memories, the daughter does not think of the photo but the event; despite only remembering things like the edges of the dark beyond the studio lights, the clean, slightly camphorous scent of the kimonos, and most of all a rustling of fabric, the solidity of material that forms a garment-nest which has been built for her. The dream of inhabiting is a reality, for it has been created to be so: by her grandmother who has made her little kimono, and her mother, who by dressing her, has placed the daughter in the space she feels safe within.

When the mother came to this country, she brought with her a tanzen, a great padded winter kimono. With its velvet collar and patchwork of fine antique silks in gold-hued olive green, navy, and burnt orange, it is never worn but lies on a bed as a thick coverlet. It is a ruin of sorts, one which straddles the worlds of specific use and disuse, for as Susan Stewart says in *The Ruins Lesson*, '. . . ruin refers to a fabric . . . that is meant to be upright but has fallen . . . what should be vertical and enduring has become horizontal and broken.' Here in this Western bedroom, the tanzen is horizontal but not broken, instead adjusting its meaning to a different world, the way the mother must and the daughter will. This is another of the daughter's earliest memories: the contrast of these ruins of paper-thin silk and dense black velvet against her baby skin, its wide weighted sleeves playfully folded over her body. Though no body ever fills it, the child regards its touch as if it were its mother, and so this mass of materials endures.

On a trip to Japan, the mother of the mother folds her new grandchild in gentle, grey kimono-clad arms on the steps of a curved bridge, showing her the koi rippling beneath. Leaning over the pond, the child wears a light blue Western dress, her baby hair the colour of the carp's orange-red scales dulled to copper under the greenish water. The grandmother has never worn Western clothes or ever left her country, but she has understood her youngest daughter's need to go elsewhere, welcoming the child of her union, a little creature regarded with curiosity by her countryfolk. The ombré of her hair and robe is another world to the cuckoo, who regards these new people and surroundings with the understanding they are hers regardless. She takes in this new world with solemn contentment and because of the kimonos she has known in that one and this, with no sense this is different from the one she has flown from. She moves from houses with numbers to houses without, their old wood and paper-framed panelled sliding doors, tatami mats, and bedding put out on the floor for the night and stored away during the day. While she has not yet formed image-memories she recognises, there is feeling: deep and wide kimono sleeves which enfold her, brush against her skin whenever she is picked up or tucked in. The daughter recalls this more than the touch of skin, the feather-light strokes of these bird-women with their cloth wings, their murmured unknown words which she translates and responds to in babbled emotions.

Jacques Derrida in *On Touching—Jean-Luc Nancy*, writes that a caress is neither demand nor possession, instead a tender gesture which only knows how to give, an ephemeral promise whose reward is to live on in the eternity of memory. In these images, to hold and touch is a gift: first as the child of a child of a child, the latter two now slowly removed by time from the state of childhood; second, as love without capital, a pure and short-lived state of freedom. For those moments of touching, both are bestowed with the absence of age and a rich and wordless communication of emotions.

In the summer backyard, the child poses by a garden chair wearing a long red cotton yukata printed with tiny white fans. The gleaming metal of her hair, now tightly plaited and coiled, is as reflective of light as her mother's is absorbing of it. One small hand flickers out from the cool sleeve like a fin; a small fish playing in the waves of Midwestern grass, an unconscious recollection of the gilded koi that swam in the Sapporo pond. In *Matter and Memory*, Henri Bergson writes, 'our daily life is spent among objects whose very presence invites us to play a part: in this the familiarity of their aspect consists.' The garment-objects of the child's life means she plays different parts; while they are both familiar to her, the audience which views her in these roles see two parts and not one person. This separation means she herself will come to be distanced from both roles and person. To play is a serious engagement, for the imaginary mimics the real and the real wishes for another reality.

The interplay of kimono and Western clothing is as much a combat at times. The daughter cannot recall being dressed in the former in Japan, and to wear one at 'home' signifies a formality with only a vague sense of identity. She likes the rough cottons and heavy silks of the robes, the mousse-like airiness of the thin silk sashes that she is bound with. Bound: not a simple wrapping and tying like shoelaces, but an elaborate winding of the long material around her still-shapeless body as she holds up her arms for eternal minutes in front of a mirror. Both she and her mother are silent, aware that this ritual is love; binding as both intimacy and creation. To wear a kimono, or even a less formal yukata, means there is time spent in and with the garment. There is a particular way to sit and a way to stand, every gesture considered but innate. No one has told her how to behave when she wears one, but her body understands. The combative feeling in her—small and angry and confused—is because she does not understand why her body understands. She knows this sense is relegated to the boundaries of the home, and to view it outside of the space becomes not a bringing together of girl and culture, but a distancing. She does not know how to contextualise this garment with her world outside of Japan, outside of the house.

Barthes, in *The Language of Fashion*, says that to understand clothing requires the knowledge that it is limitless in its expressions, a 'text without end', and so its puzzle lies in both the drawing and deciphering of its boundaries, its seams forming another kind of map. The child only understands the limits of the garment in a vague social way, and even more vaguely grasps at the question at the edges of her growing consciousness of how she is woven into this text. One day, when she is about seven or eight, her mother comes to school dressed in a kimono. She speaks to her classmates about it, and while they are polite and attentive, the girl knows this is another thing in the list of things which mark her as an interloper. She feels the hot creeping flush of an embarrassment she is ashamed of, the discord between pride and belonging whose disaffection beats loudly in her head like a parade of taiko drummers she once saw. If she understands the limits of the garment it is because there are times she wishes to cut the threads which bind her to them.

In her teenage years, she clashes with her mother frequently about clothes. It is a strange dissatisfied time, one where to be like everyone, yet different, is paramount. This warring desire and lack of clarity of who she might be, is seen to be, wants to be, manifests in how she dresses: carelessly wrapping those old silk sashes over jeans and jumpers, wearing her father's oversized gold and black jacquard haori or long indigo blue and white yukata over white t-shirts and leggings. She wears them open as a deliberate rebellion. Untying is unbinding, unbinding is unravelling, unravelling allows her to seek herself beyond the threads while acknowledging she will never cut them, an uneasy reconciliation since her childhood days. The daughter wants only to find some combination which is wholly her, to herself and to the world.

On the days she wears only Western clothes, she disappears into the dull checked linoleum of the school hallways—just one of others, but also false, for she feels whatever she wears is an attempt to be like the rest that is never quite successful. She exists in a world where one is judged on brands, the young awakening of a desire to categorise according to have and have not. The daughter belongs to the latter, and now finds that the pride which so fiercely battled with belonging in her earlier days emerges with youthful fury. She takes clothes from her mother and father and combines them with a sartorial arrogance which nonetheless masks the sting of knowing money and its display is yet another place she cannot be. But when the rough silks and cottons graze her skin, when she looks down and sees the prints of cranes and crests and patterns dancing in an elegance beyond her or anyone else's years, it is a protection different to the garment-nests of her childhood. For she now understands this armour is hers to wear in her own way, and in doing so the fledgling has started to make its own way in the world. In *Practicalities*, Marguerite Duras writes on dressing: 'a uniform is an attempt to reconcile form and content, to match what you think you look like with what you'd like to look like, what you think you are with what you want to suggest.' This is the closest she has to something that remains the same; garments which shift like a chameleon, reflecting both of the cultures she moves through.

She finds an old black and white photo of her mother as a teenager standing outside of her wooden house in the Sapporo snow, wearing a white kimono scattered with flowers, tabi and zori, her chin-length hair in a slightly waved bob. What she notices most of all is her smile: it is wide and full, and with the exception of the photo of mother and infant daughter in the photographer's studio, free of the cares that have marked the woman she has always known.

The daughter on her wedding day. In front of a mirror, she wears a cream silk dress layered beneath with tulle, wondering who it is looking back at her: this is not the place or the person she wants to be. She touches the organza of her bodice and feels constricted; it is not the same as the binding of love. When young, she played with her neighbour's dolls, their plastic limbs resistant to being dressed, and once finished lay there, waiting for their joints to be directed in unnatural movement. Discussing the poet Rilke's essay on dolls in *The Dream of the Moving Statue*, Kenneth Gross notes, 'Rilke imagines us angry and horrified when we discover . . . that stupidity of dolls that lets them be just what we liked,' their passivity and inability to interact only lost through longevity, transcending their dollness. Stiffly jointed with the fear of indecision, the daughter becomes the very doll she struggled with so long ago. Suddenly she recalls her mother's words, swimming through the ripples of silk in her memory. Hands by her sides lift halfway and drop. *I thought I was a bird.*

Galen Strawson, in *Things That Bother Me*, writes, 'grief felt for the person who has died seems like a natural expression of love, a natural expression whose absence would show failure of love.' But what of grief without the extremity of death? In her mother's snowy smile and her own wedding day reflection, the daughter feels a profound grief. She knows the latter is a failure of love; self-love, later expanding to marriage-love. With her mother, she knows it is more of an erosion: there has been nothing but love when she has known her mother, yet since that Sapporo photo, her mother has known the disintegration of a particular innocence of love which is part of the reality of its maintenance.

With the tenderness of morbidity—unpleasant subjects such as death or illness being hand-in-hand with intimacy—she sometimes wonders about the clothing of final rest. She goes through Funeral in the card catalogue of her memory and pulls up her relatives' unremarkable costumes. Only her father wore something of note, favourite tweeds which the family associated him with. Though her mother is still alive and with good fortune will continue to be, the daughter cannot help but mentally dress her for this moment. Again, Duras says, 'death, the fact of death coming towards you, is also a memory. Like the present. It's completely here, like the memory of what has already happened and the thought of what is still to come.' This dressing of a memory that has not yet occurred feels as important as imagining a doll in frozen splendour, like the kimono-clad kokeshi that lined surfaces of the house when she was young, or hinamatsuri dolls sitting in brocaded state on their tiers; passed down, and so gaining the solemnity of years, the dolls transcend the meaning of play. It is the formality of respect and the celebratory preparation of a future remembrance, the ritual of memory. She thinks again of that cream-coloured, crane and flower-adorned kimono, folded carefully in tissue and mothballs somewhere within a satin-sheen wooden chest of drawers in her childhood home. The daughter knows that her mother has had to undergo her own transformations from her childhood world to the one after her marriage. She has watched her mother shed her silken wings over time, which the child then wore and shed and then longed for again. As the years passed, she recognised the pattern of the bird-women of her life, and she now looks to her memories in the way others await the migration of the swallows.

More and more, she remembers. And when she conjures the images of wearing these garments, a strange sartorial—or perhaps it is bodily—regret appears alongside them. She reflects on a specific moment of being dressed: the feeling of the sash being bound almost across her flat child's chest. This is most likely a remnant of the infant's unformed, unarticulated comfort at being bound tightly and safely, a memory of the womb already starting to fall away. She thinks of the breasts that formed later on and her delight at their shape, which was also a delight at becoming a woman, and so belonging to *something*. As they grew larger, something her mother never had except briefly in pregnancy, she felt the distance again. The loneliness of separation from the physical attributes of an identity. She has the vagaries of an undefinable face, but her figure is Western, and she knows these curved lines would now mar the perfect geometry of what was her body in a kimono. She longs for a precise physiological equation, as if it would answer the question of herself.

She thinks again of erosion; the slow, almost unnoticeable wearing love and life can often find itself going through, a change from motion to rigidity, birds to dolls. It is not that to be the latter necessarily represents a lack of love, though it sometimes does. It is a solidity and certainty which is less evocative of nests and first flights than realising the destiny of one's eternal permanence, the transformation back to the image and dreams of the garment-house. Silk and cotton turn to wood: the grandmother, the mother, and finally the daughter in a still, smiling row, enfolded in the pinioned wings of time. The kimonos once filled with flesh and laughter and wisdom are now empty, in their dreaming folds they await new birds.

As Barthes writes in *Mourning Diary*, 'we don't forget, but something *vacant* settles in us.'

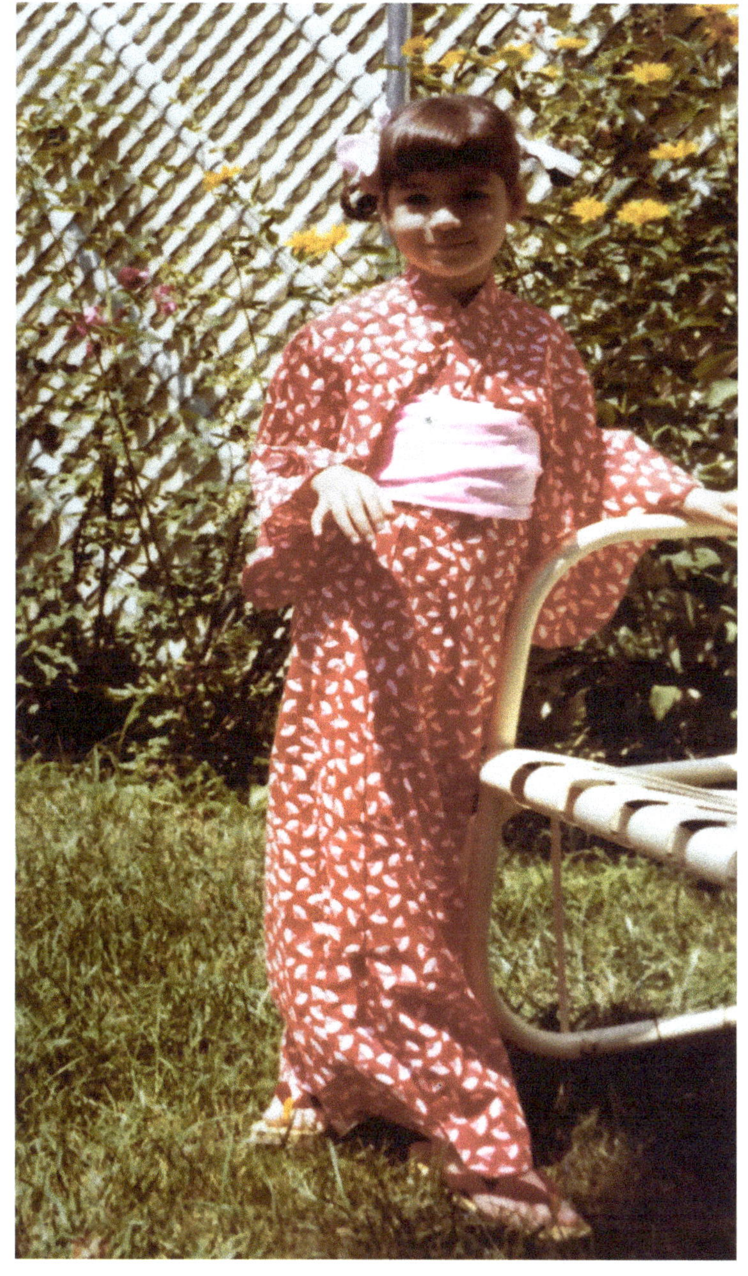

26.

A replacement game, from phrases taken at random from *Brigitte Bardot and the Lolita Syndrome* by Simone de Beauvoir:

> It is no new thing for high-minded folk to identify the flesh with sin and to dream of making a bonfire of works of art . . .
>
> They are obliged to recognize the crudity of their desire, the object of which is very precise—that body, those thighs, that bottom, those breasts.
>
> She offers herself directly to each spectator.
>
> The debunking of love and eroticism is an undertaking that has wider implications than one might think. As soon as a single myth is touched, all myths are in danger.

First, a weariness at the interchangeability of Olympia for Brigitte, or myself, or any other woman. But then there is the delight that we incur a wrath both visible and invisible for being such provocateurs—for nothing more than enduring the projections of others on our flesh while attempting to live. Specifically, I think of Victorine as Olympia in the way Brigitte is Juliette or Virginie or Camille; bearing the weight of each person's shifting fantasy dependent on character or gaze of the one who desires. These weights pile up to the point where she must assert what is the 'real' Brigitte, but what of Victorine, held down by the same, but without the testaments afforded the former? There are those, who on being presented with the mirror of their desire, would smash it rather than question what looks back. What one wants, one invariably destroys. The result is destruction of anything pertaining to the flesh but also beyond it; a separate self, any response which does not mimic one imagined by the one who desires. It is a reminder that sin is not flesh but an inability to reconcile desire with humanity. The point of a bonfire of the vanities is the fanatical love of its flames.

27.

Michel, I must confess I laughed when you spoke of ' the creature' of Hoffmann's 'The Sandman', for you do not explicitly speak her name, while I have whispered it to myself repeatedly since I was young, first obsessed with the story of the young man in love with the doll-woman. Olimpia! Olympia! Why is it that no one thinks of her words, the only ones she can utter: 'Ah, ah', says Olympia, as did I once, waiting to come alive, not yet knowing it was within my own power to do so. Those are old words which I cast aside once, revived upon reading your remembrance of her. It was then I recalled again the automaton I was. Not 'an ornament with no soul', but a soul without its own shell. There are two skins to every story, that of flesh and wood or metal, paint or loneliness; it hardly matters. I can feel my teeth set hard against each other when I think you and Nathaniel look at your Olympias as things to be brought to life by your desires—both the same Olympia, white and mute and ornamental, fit for rescue but never escape.

28.

To think of her, draped in her flowers, is to also consider shunga (spring pictures), Japanese erotic ukiyo-e art. Both celebrated and censored, it is the literal expression of the fantasies projected on Olympia's flesh-canvas, the meaning of the flowers which adorn and surround her. Are such things in the blood? Without being shown or told, was there something in those woodcuts and paintings likewise carved, stroked into a sense, passed down and down through my mother's line, emerging in me as an innate understanding this binding of pleasure and art and womanhood was part of me? To grow up without the shame and weight which so often accompanies the discovery of sexuality is a freedom. It allows a child to view both such artworks with frankness: the ability for pictures to be not just representative of their notoriety—which comes much later—but also the true essence of what it is to gaze, a kaleidoscopic, telescopic viewing of an entire world, a galaxy. If you had told me Olympia or shunga was but a kind of star, remote and removed from others in its particular qualities, how could I possibly then want to know of the rest of the world or how to go about reaching it? They would forever be things alone, and each other thing I encountered, I would consider as another separate thing. To a child, everything in the world must be able to be connected, first within the realm of their own logic, that of the world's following. Oftentimes the latter is not a better logic, for the conclusions to their hypotheses may be functional but not ideal, whereas the logic of a child allows for the ideal, never quite as concerned for the functional, yet happier for it. For all the scrutiny sex falls under, it is true that shunga as it translates describes everything about sex as an ideal: blossoms, growth, newness, a state of nature which at its apotheosis connects the world. To a child viewing a woman, a man, a scene: nothing shocks, for she, too, has a body. Unlike the ones she views, to be sure, but a body nonetheless. The gaze is of wonder and curiosity, the same gaze which is turned to subjects of art adults would call at least superficially mundane (Cezanne's apples), or horrific (Goya's Saturn). The act may be for now meaningless, the display of the body viewed without prejudice, but this only serves to bring other beauty to the forefront: a fold of cloth, a pattern, the angle of a glance which looks at someone within the frame or without. The child consumes all to process both now and later, the formation of synapses which one day will create a galaxy, and in doing so, ensures nothing in it remains alone.

29.

It is difficult to see the pearl which is suspended at the heart of the ribbon's bow, itself at the centre of the hollow of Olympia's throat, without thinking of its precarious state: a suspended raindrop whose perfect form is dependent on stillness, just as a cat's bell only benefits the creature if it never chases its prey. But we know such passivity has no part in the greater scheme of nature: the raindrop is destined to break and saturate the skin or earth, the cat must heed its instinct and try to catch its bird or mouse. What impatience is it which Olympia frustrates and is frustrated by, held back by her statue's controlled pose and fixed breathing?

30.

Sometimes I forget that you are not here, Michel, and that is testament to what you are—for you *are* with me—hoping for in writing, 'my way of existing in the minds of strangers, allows me to stretch the limits of my mortal self'. Is this writing simply a denial, or a realisation that still insists on pushing away a death that comes yet a few paces closer with each passing year? Perhaps what starts as ego, a climber confident in attempting the highest peak, becomes what all things are reduced to: an act which records a survival-in-progress, the contradictory wish of immortality. What does it mean to start as I have, knowing that arm's length was my Virgil? Never having thought I existed in the minds of others (this explains my relative content over the years having conversations within my head) now I find I am occasionally seized—always at night, when the body reminds the sleepless of its unrelenting schedule which waits for no one's grand plans—with an urgency to decipher my own meaning, this externalisation a proof of life for anyone else who cares to know I am alive; but most of all, from myself.

31.

You and I have always been travelling to this particular destination, Michel. I first saw Olympia as a child, a collection of books on the great museums on a bookshelf in my childhood bedroom. She struck me even then, the recognition of simple flesh before more complex carnal knowledge, the first of a stop on a journey which would entwine image and words, even though I could not know then where it was I was going. But she has always been there, in the way your fragments floated through my head, a voice in search of a form.

32.

At any rate, I was spared the cliché of Olympia rendering me breathless, for I was already literally so. In the throes of the aftermath of an asthma attack as a child, which then would last at least a week, I would spend all my time in bed, unable to sleep lying down. Propped with pillows, I would sit and view the world from a hunched-back perspective—aware of the constant presence of a ragged breath more appropriately belonging to someone at the opposite of the spectrum of life—which narrowed everything I knew to a single bedroom. That bookshelf became the world; I travelled accordingly. Olympia was tenderness before all else, the sick-nurse propped on her couch in solidarity. Flowers of my own were printed on a pillowcase: buttercups, Queen Anne's lace, bluebells, cowslips. My attendant mother standing by with a bouquet of mandarins, feeding me its petal-segments one by one.

33.

Would she have been as shocking if it were not for those deliberately careless half-adornments which speak of the audacity of debauchery much more than the body? The ribbon of course, but also the flower, earrings, bracelet, the fringed shawl beneath her warm from body heat, imploring to be pulled away, the silk or satin boudoir slippers half-on, half-off. Even the sombre green draperies reveal a glimpse to the voyeur—or perhaps it is she who will turn in a moment and look, like an animal or Diana in the forest, wary of intrusion. Olympia is *almost*: naked, indecent, possessed. A symbol of sexual liminality, the *no* as *maybe*, the *maybe* as *yes*. The half-filled glass, the yellow light. Obsession reads uncertainty as its opposite, and so to the possessive, Violette Leduc's words call out from every object: 'disorder is surrender: we want to set things free'.

34.

'There is no ideal body for a nude. It's all in the context in which it's seen' said the '70s fashion photographer Chris von Wangenheim, whose images were seen as straddling, often crossing the line from risqué into alarm. I think about this when I consider what you say about the word 'porno', the impenetrability of it, as opposed to the flowing invitation of it in its entirety—and above all, who will free it. Now, more than painting, it is the lens which has freed both the word and the woman, a frame that forces a multiplicity of perspectives even when it, too, is enflamed by the illusion of one. Von Wangenheim's 'Woman Behind Chain Link Fence' features the tragically short-lived model Gia Carangi standing nude behind a fence, hands clasped over her intimacy in an aggressive but beguiling gesture which makes me think she is the rightful heir to Olympia's gaze. The title of photo deliberately misleads: Gia might be *seen* as behind the fence and therefore a prisoner, but von Wangenheim himself writes in a 1980 essay about his work that the fence was a prop held in place by assistants; a movable bias. Her look is both at the viewer and beyond, the unnerving feeling that anyone before her can be seen through with ease, the stare of Olympia. Her standing pose is the progression of freedom, the movement from horizontal to vertical that echoes Jean-Léon Gérôme's *Truth Coming Out of Her Well*; a warning that women are coming to be seen, seen to be coming. Apt when considering the life of Carangi, whose appetites undeniably led in part to her untimely death, she nevertheless represented a woman who refused to be unchecked by sexual mores, still shocking in the hedonistic late '70s and early '80s. As a friend of hers noted, 'Gia and I would go out . . . she loved to get fucked up the ass with fingers and that horrified me, so she talked about it more.' Words remain this powerful for us, still impure in our mouths to some: you may imagine us in a future sexual act or capture us in a present one, but nothing inflames as much as the *utterance*, whether falling from our lips or from our fingers as we write, for it makes our pleasure real without you. For all the eyes that took in Olympia and Gia creating fantasy images, myths, and cautionary tales from their bodies, they forget that in the beginning was the word, and the word they dared not speak was cunt. What lies behind their hands has lit the world, Michel—that is why there is fire.

35.

The cat; you nearly forget, one pussy—despite being tantalisingly unrevealed, 'the intimate muff concealed'—overwhelming another. I wonder if the photographer Jeanloup Sieff laughed when he shot the 1973 photo 'Chat solitaire dans un décor inhospitalier' as I did when I saw it; the cat sitting in the chair luxuriating in the solidity of its solitude, but just as intent on who it is gazing at them.

36.

There are times when you speak of the sexual act which make me think of nothing so much as a male peacock, fluttering and preening. After the words and thoughts are exhausted, there is still the show, and despite all the eloquent descriptions of Olympia as a prostitute, fantasy, doll, performer, here you are revealing in your own timid striptease—

for you merely describe taking out your cock, while the woman is imagined as a circus performer—that you would like nothing more than to be the same. Do I laugh? Sometimes. I like it when others recognise it themselves, for sex understood as funny and awkward takes on a human intimacy that is oftentimes removed by all in an attempt to remove the animal from the act. But what are we really but those glorious birds in the mating dance? And while we alone have the ability to create *more*, a space of pleasure between simple reproduction and pornography—if we define the latter as emotionless as the former, which I do not—we still fear both and remain wary of what could be. Forever pinned under the ruins of guilt, religion, expectation; able to imagine all possible worlds but this one. There was once a model, a beautiful Nordic creature who inexplicably turned his eyes to me. Naturally flattered and curious at bedding something resembling divinity, I went willingly to him. But before that came the very show I speak of: he stroked his hard, hairless body with a tenderness that did not require me, then stalked the room, arousing himself in a sexual parade which left me a bird-watcher more than an evening mate. The act itself left me feeling curiously as if I were surplus to requirement, he a Narcissus bedding his own reflection. And so I did what any Olympia would do and seized my own pleasure: imagining lovers past and future, the images of bodies, painted and photographed which so intrigued me—hers among them—brought myself to orgasm underneath that blond god, soaking his sheets in an act which declared *I was here*, with the satisfaction he was as unnecessary as I.

37.

In your wordplay you move from 'enribbon' to 'inseminate'—is everything to be about the possession of her? I am hesitant of playing, consciously or unconsciously choosing words like cards and seeing how they may fall. But in my head the game has already started.

You first: enribbon, encircle, enclose.

My turn: the loop, a capture. In rodeo, breakaway roping, where a calf is released before the rider attempts to lasso it. Kinder than tying it down afterwards, but still nothing but a hunt which, necessarily, benefits only the hunter. You speak of this yourself but I wonder, do we have the stomach to let go of the ribbon-rope which has ensnared both of us and Olympia?

Start again: embed, enroot, insert, enrich.

And: bulb, iris, hyacinth, blood. Open, devour. I came across a recipe for pickled hyacinth bulbs, once thought by the ancients to be an aphrodisiac, at the same time remembering that the flowers bloomed where the blood of Hyacinthus, Apollo's lover, was spilled.

Once more: illumine, enlighten, inflame, inseminate.

And: no words, only an image: a 1971 photograph of Isabelle Weingarten by Serge Lutens. Drained of blood, instead dressed in its tint down to her nails and winged eye makeup, she lifts one hand above her head, the other to her mouth as if to utter a battle cry, both breathing and devouring the magenta-pink flames which radiate from her hidden mouth. The title of the piece: 'Cracheuse de flammes'.

Shall we play again, Michel?

38.

Annoyed at the renewed panic over the question of whether to own many books is a mark of deficiency or degeneracy in a person, I turn instead to the question of why one persistence of modernity is the idea that a person should necessarily, and ironically, be less attached to an old symbol en masse—not least because it indicates an unseemly preference over society—while at the same time be more dependent on the infinite new devices and avenues that are meant, in theory, to unify people and cultures (the result of its practice appears no better or worse—though immediacy leans towards the latter—than any other attempt in bringing disparate humans together). Certainly one may accumulate people in the way others do books, for the sheer number and the accompanying sense of value; a false one, though what a person allows themselves to believe is no less true until the point where it is no longer the case. But it also strikes me that the answers around the justification of collection, which is not often collection as a conscious, regulated activity, circle around the banal—most likely because it is difficult to qualify love in a unique way and the dissenters around the devoted activity of book purchasing and collection require an explanation it is admittedly hard to find language for. We understand love as an articulate, complex emotion, whereas the language for it is reduced to simplifications, at which point we reach for metaphor, the last resort of the speechless. This is something I, too, freely admit, for in attempting to justify to myself the shelves of books randomly acquired over the long years—there being, like love, dry spells and times where one fixates on a particular quality or subject in the object of one's adoration—it seems most direct to say, I enjoy having the wealth of knowledge at my immediate disposal, perhaps being the child of a librarian and growing up in a house of books besides, but the truth is it is something more along the lines of building a city, where one looks at the space available—I mean mental not physical, so spaces as subjects of interest—and then builds streets and bridges, houses and buildings, parks and transportation lines accordingly; after which, one has the pleasure of becoming both resident and tourist of this metropolis. This might appear to some as a supreme act of ego, but then what great or small acts in the outside world are not, in any sense of the word? If it is a case of control, then that again is something which has always been hand in hand with accomplishment—any purposeful one. And if it is a case of degeneracy or deficiency, then we must ask ourselves what markers of this have remained constant since the beginnings of our species—the answer is, very few, which then becomes a mere trend in the perspective of behaviour. If it is selfishness, then I point to writing, both a selfish and selfless act. Selfish in that it is hardly altruistic, but at the same time, it is a communal act: unless it never sees light of day, its purpose becomes one of reaching out—whether conscious or not. So the collection of books, this act of internal urban planning, is in a small way the intimate act of the propagation of the self: its possibilities, ideas, and people it has come into contact with, paper dandelions whose seeds are blown out of the mind and into the world.

39.

Now, the abundance of flesh—as strong a currency as ever in the world—at our disposal renders Olympia superfluous. The meanings of her pose, her gaze, her nudity, all too simplistic for a time which demands our existence be equal to a body mapped in trauma, a butcher's diagram where one might select the choicest cuts. If our bodies once filled galleries, they now fill bestiaries; we move from gaze to moral lesson as we always have. The body holds a being, and if we were trapped by one viewpoint then we are still trapped by another now, unable to be more than a pound of flesh. The present forgets the past like a new wind which does not recognise the grasses of a previous season. It rewrites and refigures trying to create a new relevance, ignoring what Susan Stewart says so bluntly:

> the trauma is a product of its repetition.

and,

> we should remember that the very first defining trait of the trauma is its 'intensity', the degree to which it resists incorpo-

ration into the economy of the subject and so incapacitates the subject.

It becomes difficult to find the delineation between the relaying of trauma in art and writing, the deliberate trapping of experiences in a loop whereby the body retains a relevancy it may no longer have outside of the traumatic experience, and the attempt to break free of it; to write beyond or through, any means which presents a path out of this particular maze. Fear now rests not in the experience or scrutiny of its representation but in the possibility that it is not enough for observations of interest, and if there is no interest, then we must not exist to others; if we do not exist for them, how do we justify solitude to ourselves separate to a shock of which now functions as a means of socialisation and validation? We are left with an instinctual grasping in the dark in terms of how we see our bodies represented and what we are describing when we (re)create them and their experiences: are we original or merely forgeries? It leaves me wanting to take a marker to Olympia and divide her body in a different way: where is your happiness, your desire, the thoughts that none of us imagined you held in your depths? But they were always there, invisible, beneath the complexity of being a traumatic object—where sentience, however remote, is irrelevant to its aesthetic status; the body may be or have been real, what is projected onto it may not be in the sense that the body has not experienced it, but it remains a truth because it is what is generally understood in viewing it. Olympia's body has never been separate from the scrutiny associated with negative sexuality, where sexuality can only be regarded as a moral binary, the rules of its two halves determined by someone other than the object. But in a parallel regard, she is as relevant now as she was then, outside of this aesthetic trauma. It is only that no one asked her or me about our dreams, our fantasies, and pleasures; what creates the whole instead of what divides, what we give to and take from the world rather than only what is taken from us, the tectonic shift that moves us from being seen as a field of identical blooms to a singular flower.

40.

I envy those able to write without the pall of the present drawing its veil over their words. But as you say, Michel, 'the past in ruins, the present in disarray, the future in tatters'. Sometimes when I read your words I wonder if you felt the same trepidation I feel writing these, seeing the page with a dulled eye, hearing thoughts with a 'discordant ear', even the fingers somehow belonging to another, slightly numbed from the morning's news already putrefying good intentions, the sickly-sweet stench in my olfactory memory of infection seeping through my pores. Someone told me a strange tale the other day about flatworms, on being sectioned, retaining the memory-gestures of the original, little copies burdened with the same history. Despite our hubris when it comes to the idea we are individual, it becomes harder to push away the feeling that experiences are as likely to resurface in others, a facsimile of process to close to an incestuous bind. As you say 'the past, pierced by so many memory holes', I remember again of my childhood obsession with Mantegna's *St. Sebastian*—for if obsessed with that saint, it necessarily follows that mania will take different forms as one develops, not just sexually, but as a result of the slow weights of aging and time tethering both the body and mind. The crux of that obsession was faith: not in divinity but the desire for a similar heart which would transcend any shaft of pain or break in one's (then) small world. But to return to these 'memory holes', no arrow could be truer in its path than my immediate recollection of Byung-Chul Han on memory and scent: 'scents . . . are able to stabilize a self that is threatened with dissociation by providing it with a framing identity, an image of self.' What holds us together when the fabric of the world seems beyond repair, knowing that rents in it will, by association, leave us in tatters? I always return to scent, for whenever I think of a memory responsible for a fracture, there was always a corresponding one which functioned as an olfactory balm. Even death—and you yourself mention 'trying to find some charm in its perfume'—had its scents, such as Guerlain Eau Impériale, the cologne my father was buried with, or a tin of gelatinous mink oil, for I remember polishing a pair of brown leather shoes when my young cousin was dying, its mild glycerine-petrol fragrance soothing my anxieties into something akin to white noise, static and numbing. There is a perfumed oil called Aftelier Ancient Resins, created for Leonard Cohen, made with frankincense and Balm of Gilead, which has always made me wonder if this too, was conceived as a scented heart he could turn to. Deliberately more tangible and sensual than the divine, acting as censer for our memories, our bodies exuding trails of holy smoke even as our eyes look upwards; consumed with the trinity of past, present, and future.

41.

In a brief essay on the photography of Serge Lutens, the choreographer Ushio Amagatsu says 'obsession is important in art . . . we could say that first there is the body, then dialogue'. It is so with Olympia: not simply because first and foremost her body *is* the canvas, but because body responds to body as an innate communication; specifically, the will to connection where connection is intimacy. Amagatsu again: 'to look at a picture, it is the body that first chooses to stop'. Before the mind there is instinct, a preternatural observation which may or may not give us pause. What comes next can be fluid or stopped short by extraneous checkpoints of morality. What if Olympia's gaze had been downcast, or off in the distance, rather than directly at the viewer? Perhaps, then, she would be of no importance, the body as broken circuit: unable to communicate, mutely subservient to a form. When I recall life drawing classes, most of our models did not interact, frozen into their poses for however long—ten, twenty minutes, a half hour. They looked down or away—even dozed—though it was the rare few who would talk and watch the students drawing, despite perfectly holding their poses, which created an unnerving atmosphere: living statuary that somehow made me think of what might have happened if Pygmalion's Galatea had instead been indifferent to his caress. When I look at Olympia I think of the original shock of her, the model as creation who dared to looked back. Clad in nothing but flesh and ornaments, she provokes those who wish her to be viewed—taken—in silence; confronted instead with a dialogue, a conversation of two voices rather than the communication of one.

42.

If Olympia speaks through us, Michel, why should I not ask her to speak through the most modern of modernities, that of AI? I showed her image to the *I Magma* app, the interactive work of artist Jenna Sutela with Memo Akten and Allison Parrish, which through images fed to it by the user, 'builds a bridge between these ancient systems of knowledge and our contemporary attempts to divine the future. It's within this assemblage of data and matter that Sutela posits the potential for a new collective consciousness driven by magma. This primordial 'goo' becomes both the physical 'grey matter' that flows within a series of head-shaped lava lamps and the data driven lava of the app, powering the flow of the oracle's predictions'.

Sibyl meet sibyl—the camera eye scans Olympia's body, turquoise blue lava bubbles rising and drifting across her flesh, dividing her into not one, but two Olympias. For a moment, the silence of its deliberation, then came forth:

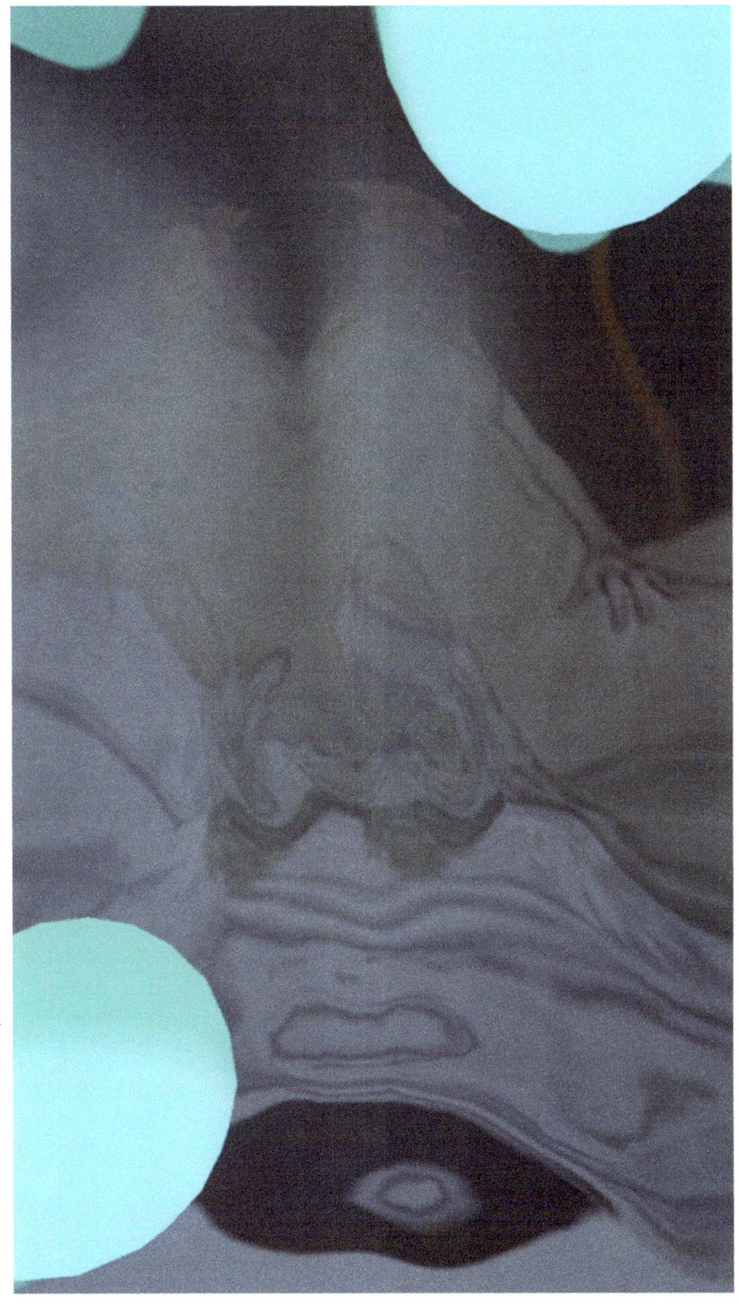

'and ecstasies learned of the host, without rage'

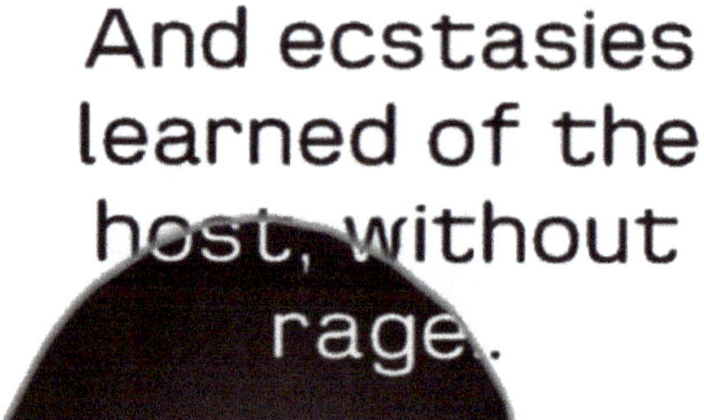

Was this Olympia's surreptitious pleasure in her receipt of neverending gaze, the delight in observing the observer? Without rage: her expression translated repeatedly but always yielding a different response: calm, amusement, tolerance, pity. But *without rage*—the stillness of the host in the eye of entertainment, patient until the last guest has departed.

A second plea. This time, cascading shapes of darker blues and greens, before its utterance:

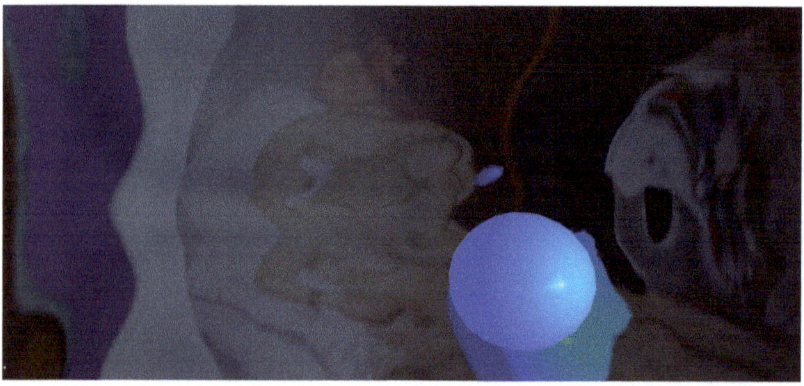

'I went out to endure'

I went out to endure

Ah, ah, Olympia! So you did, so you continue to do; our questions and fantasies, written and whispered to you, endured like the love for your sister Olimpia, both created for a purpose not your own: to lure in near-silence, gather the eyes and voices which come to pay homage or murmur wishes which can never be fulfilled. But you go on, living in your singular way, outliving us all, until the time when only Olimpia and Olympia remain, sisters in earned solitude.

43.

As children beginning school, like the little primitives we were, knowledge was not something we took in merely as receiving the breath of another. We smelled and touched and tasted more than we listened and looked, small creatures looking for possible nourishment in each object we found before us. It was in an art class that we especially realised this. A loud instinct invited us to explore, and our teacher, a woman obsessed with Georgia O'Keeffe's flower and desert paintings, indulged us under her eyes, as large and blue as the artist's morning glories. And so we feasted on the materials presented like courses of a grand meal: the high bitterness of small white cups of tempera which mimicked undrinkable cups of 2am coffee we would discover as adults, and the disappointing blandness of watercolours like beautiful but unseasoned soups. Waxy, silken chalk sticks of candy-coloured crayons and pastels crumbled and snapped with unparalleled satisfaction between our teeth and fingers, while wet and dry lumps of red-brown clay reminded us of the smell of turned gardens and parched earth in the height of summer. Ravenous, we ate and destroyed and absorbed a roomful of colour in the understanding this was how you came to know the world.

44.

Looking at my desk, littered with the wreckage of bodies, scents, and time, fragments from an old life and a new one—vintage advertisements for perfumes ('Les parfums des fourrures WEIL Paris', 'Wear Réplique, drive him wild'); a Pommery Louise 2004 champagne cork from some anniversary or celebration; a small hourglass; an overflowing pen holder; a Klein blue paper woman's torso with gilded intimacies; a wooden bowl filled with cables; a replica vintage Olivetti Lettera 22 poster still rolled; partially burned candles (Diptyque Menthe Verte and Astier de Villatte Québec, a sweetgrass fragrance); omamori pouches hanging round the necks of stone dogs that top a pair of Chinese seals, I see clearly for the first time the large framed picture which sits on the centre's edge. Nothing technically remarkable, a life drawing sketch of a woman on a crumpled piece of brown paper. Nevertheless, it pleased me, reminding me of my brief foray at art school. In a walking pose, her body is fashioned from a cacophony of wild black lines edged in white to capture light. Around her neck, a red string, cord, ribbon; untied, it drapes round her breast and wrist, dropping to the floor in a coil. The white and the red again, Olympia undone: where does that length go? The model's head, devoid of features but looking forward, leading herself out of what labyrinth? It seems unthinkable to imagine Olympia's ribbon without its strict closure, which somehow tethers her to both the frame and the onlooker, now trailing down her body as if suggesting to the viewer her fixture upon that bed was transient; that in a moment she would remove the black trail beyond the painting's boundaries, away from all eyes. In a supreme moment of self-love removing herself from where she lay, an attempted sacrifice to desire, into the impenetrable depths of the labyrinth. Only the cat follows the ribbon, which now undone, allows it to finally play with its mistress.

45.

Queen on her own colour. She remembers her father teaching her how to play chess, something that must have been as frustrating as attempting to get a kitten to do tricks, being as she was, not even five years old. Every so often in her life she had stopped and looked back in wonder, trying to figure out how he went about instilling the ideas of logic and observation in a child without obvious lessons. Then, in the middle of the night, as these bursts of realisation often come, she thought it must have been the chess board itself: the particular repetition he impressed upon her in showing her where each piece had its place, its abilities, and limitations. Sixty-four squares, each with new perspectives depending on what piece rested on it. The game was incidental: the trick was showing her how to look without telling her what to look for or where, the embedding of the board in her mental vision whenever she looked out at the world. But it was the queen that always stood out, his impressing of her vast potential upon the girl's small person: what does she see, where does she go, who can she capture.

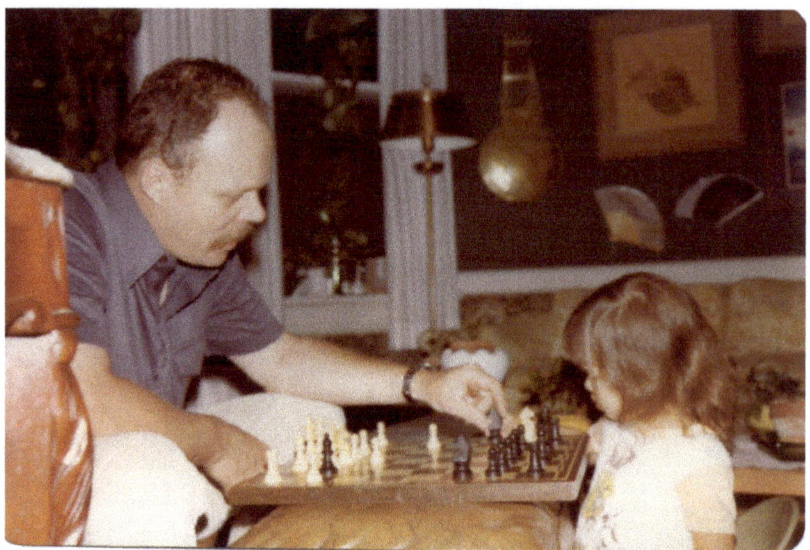

46.

Olympia, the centre of a triptych between Ingres' *Grande Odalisque* and Titian's *Venus of Urbino*. The concubine, the prostitute, and the goddess all a reminder of the Guerilla Girls poster declaring: 'Do women have to be naked to get into the Met. Museum?' *You don't have to be naked but it helps*, something which appears in my head every time I start to write, the past urging of others which was a lesson in what I should not be and what I was expected to be; neither allowing for who I was. What is a creation that does not acknowledge its materials? Flesh is as much that as paint and words. Olympia startles because one has the impression of a will subtly making itself known: her head held stiff, not languid and malleable the way the odalisque's turns back, or the seductive droop of Venus's, both yielding without hesitation. Olympia's stiffness is stubbornness. It is the denial of a mind when the body must be given, a sentiment of obstinacy echoed in Louise Bourgeois's *Sainte Sébastienne* with her exaggerated Venus of Willendorf-like curves, ringed and headless like a felled tree—*mark my ages and my experience*, she says. Shot through with arrows which point accusingly at the desired flesh, both hers and others: stomach, breasts, thighs, calves, cunt. The fat of the land, plundered. Bodies which have been manipulated for too long, but continue to be.

47.

I lost my voice at six. Not the physical inability to speak, but the will or wish to do so. What retreats I had previously made into my head were the result of my asthma; now the sticky scent of illness was outside of the body, the strangeness of being so completely aware of a social displacement that was the result of looking and, with the cruel logic of suspicion, seeming so different to the children around me. Asked to read aloud a few lines in a little group, I started, and froze. The lines were describing the noises of musical instruments, the alien sounds suddenly confirming my own status as an alien—not in the governmental sense, but of a child on the outskirts of other children, the most distancing thing of all. I started again, froze again, my lips unable to persuade the requisite sounds to emerge, though in my head I was speaking freely with childish eloquence. On starting one more time I burst into tears instead, the wild contrast of them with the silence of the rest of the classroom, unable to tell if it was their sympathy or greater distance that hung heavy over me. The incident marked a withdrawal from the world; not the taking of vows in any sense, but the safety of an interiority which allowed for all, the opposite of the world with which I continued to reluctantly interact. In turning away it had the irony of opening the world to me; to play and look and indulge any desires and thoughts I might have been required to place before a tribunal of my peers for approval, a decadence of which I became increasingly aware was a freedom, held back as we are by the rules and judgements of others. Solitude yielded such pleasures of knowledge and knowledge of pleasure—among them, writing to myself and others: what a relief it is to read you saying 'a wandering stroll taken by thought . . . the event becomes writing', a thing I could not yet articulate but both doubted and trusted in my young self—it would be hard of me to look back on that long period before I became an adult with any anguish—or much, for I also cannot deny the scar of that particular memory is as flinching and fresh as the day I stood in the corner of the classroom, book in hand, confused tears sliding down my face.

48.

Maps of violence, Michel—in reading of your fracas in the rue Dauphine, I recall my own observation of a fight that broke out in front of me not that far away on the Quai Voltaire, on the way to an exhibition. As with such events, I missed its beginning, only realising at a point a few wide pavement stones away, two men were violently fighting. To say violently may seem superfluous, but I have often enough witnessed those near-altercations where two people do not quite dare to cross the invisible threshold, their anger projected ghost-like into the air while their bodies remain stiff and confused as whether to follow. It must have been some petty traffic squabble, as one man was a cyclist, knocked off his bicycle by the driver of a car the latter had abandoned in order to pursue what he deemed his offender. Like chess pieces tired of their polite war, the men occupied the same wide stone square, pushing and taking swings at each other, while passers-by attempted to separate them. What is it that makes us stand and watch such a spectacle? I felt as I always do at any verbal or physical confrontation, off-balance, a knot in the pit of my stomach. After a few moments I crossed to the other side of the street, but I confess for one sickening—for I was repulsed by how strong a desire it was—second I wanted to enter the fray, in the way some people have an irrational desire to drive off a bridge they are crossing or into an oncoming lane of cars. If I am honest I do not care to know what it is inside of us which triggers that if not death wish, then one of unbearable extremity, other than I have supposed it mostly lies dormant, waiting for the moments where it becomes of actual use, shedding our lifetime of learned civilities in the name of self-preservation. I know a sleeping rage lies inside of me, for I have felt its nervous itch around the edges of my everyday mannerisms since I was young, unable to neither indulge nor dismiss it. 'What do you think you're looking at? You go to hell!' Something in me knows I am your antagonist of the rue Dauphine as well as both those sparring men in the street, just a moment's walk away from the eyes of Olympia. A shoulder waiting for a chip, redress for a world which has always acted with impunity.

49.

A humorous interlude. I pick up J-K Huysmans' *Parisian Sketches* and turn to what I think is a random page. The title which greets me tells me every inch of my unconscious is filled with Olympia:

> THE ARMPIT
>
> *For Guy de Maupassant*

Its sensory and sensual musings find yet more connection. Huysmans writes the most intimate disclosure of the scent of the Parisienne's underarm in the urban heat of its seasons and society. 'Her scent escapes, ameliorated by the filter of her underclothes, at one and the same time both deliciously impudent and shyly delicate!' I look at Olympia again, her right arm angled in such a way on the tower of pillows to give the merest glimpse for those with another kind of fetish, and although her eyes are wide open, I imagine the suggestion of a wink. A scent from my own skin disorders my thoughts, making me think it is *her* I smell; Divine's L'être Aimé, with its spice of sandy intimate flesh too long exposed to the lazy heat of a day lost in the sun.

50.

The nearly imperceptible movement of the undulating wave, the sway of insect's antennae. A lip reddened and swollen only to the lover's eye, the fine rising hairs of a voyeur's arm. The quiver of an ear instinctually recognising your 'intimate resonance', the memory of skin and salt on the tip of a tongue bathed in the first drops from a pink sea. The heat of a conversation whose embers still inflame the mind, and the animal scent of an imagined connection. Any word I choose from your list, Michel, whether 'glow', 'pulsate', or 'odorize', brings me back to the sensory fury which Olympia demands. You ask for the invented word to describe your pages, but there is none, nor should there be for mine. Our attempts at painting Olympia after paint are an ephemerality like the smell of smoke after a blown-out match, a presence in the room which fills us with longing: to light the world in order to hold on to the fleeting moment. These pages should disappear after reading, only the senses left aflame as a reminder it is what is does not remain which we pursue like the half-remembered dream.

51.

Renée from Emile Zola's *La Curée* comes several years after the Manet. Reeking of near-incest and corrupted ennui, the origin of an echo Jean Baudrillard recognises when later speaking of the Santa Barbara wealthy: 'what do you do when everything is available—sex, flowers, the stereotypes of life and death?' Whether in the artificial tropic of a poison garden or the pink and grey shell of a boudoir fit for a Venus from hell, she is the remaindered pleasure of forbidden exploration, the shored wreck of the weather of men. Olympia, in her clever way, gives away nothing: who knows if she is bored, exhausted by sex; not necessarily the act but the idea that she must be its ideal, a figure in tableaux vivants that never really change. Sylvia Plath unwittingly recalls Renée's ennui and Olympia's pose later in *The Bell Jar* with the beautiful sun-lounging women of the Amazon hotel, bored of their experiences of men and their money, bored of the flowers and the waiting, but waiting nevertheless, because that is the frame that allows them to continue to be the picture of desire. But *unlike* Olympia, there is nothing in their eyes that longs fiercely for a world beyond what is available. Everyone knows—then and now—the ones society calls whores aren't nearly so as much as the ones we call respectable.

52.

What is the name of the flower with its nearly-vulgar vegetal flesh, fixed so prominently in Olympia's hair? What the hand conceals, the ear displays. The matching blush in her cheeks, tint of her lips and nipples further inviting the question of what lies hidden but never answering; the hermaphroditic orchid, keeping close its male and female elements within its velvet drapery. When you speak of 'rose and floral folds', the room is suddenly fragrant, and though I know you mean the colour rose-pink, it is roses which I smell nevertheless: not the spiced, woody rose perfumes I prefer, instead, a cloudburst of petals downy-soft but overwhelmingly redolent to match what she keeps out of sight—what else but the bouquet of Yves Saint Laurent Paris? The designer's olfactory love letter to the city is the same song as the one we sing about Olympia. She holds her palm, fingers spread, flat with a resolute arrogance. Like the impatience of a waved fan, sometimes she becomes a little cock, at others a coquette. Renée's hothouse orchids and jaded appetite. The splayed bloom of Gustave

Courbet's *L'Origine du monde* a year after the Manet, an orchid with no face. Olympia, not so much a flower as inflorescence; perpetually blooming in the heat of obscenity.

53.

Syncope #2: age seventeen, walking up the stairs to her apartment, she collapses gently upon a step, knees together, arms stretched out as if she were giving herself in a balletic, submissive pose. But her eyes close for a minute or two and then there is nothing but a blank black canvas before she raises her head again, as Alain Badiou says, 'black is the sign of the offering of an object . . . whiteness undefended'. After a brief sleep Briar-Rose emerges from a bed of cheap red carpet. Looking down at her hands, for a confused moment thinking the blood has drained from her veins, seeping into the dirty fibres. She used to drive past a vast factory with her father which emitted great clouds of grey smoke, a musty, earthy smell like potting soil; *horse blood—fertilizer*, he would say, eyes on the road. She never knew if it was true. Blood to feed, blood to grow. Closing the door behind her, she looks into the bathroom mirror and sees the blank of her face, veiled in white like the first time. Realising she is starting to bleed she lies back on the sofa, the same one which her photographer boyfriend will take pictures of her for his project, *Beauty*. Transformed into abstract curves and lines of black and white but no suggestion of a face with its fugitive red, she considers it an incomplete image of herself. As she will recall reading Badiou years later, she felt her body withdrawing into unknowing even as it offered itself.

54.

'There's an abyssal bliss in resisting lucid excuses for visual phenomena . . . don't fight it' says the critic Martin Herbert in an essay on the artist Paola Pivi. Earlier, he writes briefly on the human necessity for narrative before elaborating about why the standard applications of such validations—for what else is narrative if not a way to will a self of some kind into existence—do not apply to Pivi. In describing her work *It's a Cocktail Party*, an installation of what could be reductively described as industrial fountains without a purposeful purpose, he writes:

> The senses are asked to process simultaneously the pleasures of color, an interface of organicism and mechanism, compound scents, order and disorder, and the very fact that the stories we tell to process it won't hold.

After reading this, it becomes almost impossible to consider any hitherto accepted viewing of Olympia: her 'shocking' modernity, the supposed frank look of the prostitute, becomes the easiest explanation and therefore the one that sticks, despite feeling instinctually wrong, a facet which has been burdened with the work of a whole. It is no coincidence that the writer Edith Wharton has her social pariah Lily Bart proclaim 'what is truth? where a woman is concerned, it's the story that's easiest to believe'. But a particular pleasure and necessity of looking at Olympia now is to view her as if she were a Surrealist creation: *this is not Olympia*—at least, not the woman we have known, and it is true that we have never even known that woman. A myriad of Olympias, distilled to different essences as if she were a flower at the hands of a manic perfumer, and so within the bottle-frame, transformed: a subversive, literal objectification, the object becoming more powerful in its multiplication. As Herbert suggests with Pivi, the processing of pleasure becomes a disorder of the senses which allows for new and multiple narratives to run riot.

Olympia, reimagined: Manet's painting vanished, in its place four rooms each holding a frame enclosing a blank black canvas. Different perfumes fill the rooms as the viewer reads the name and description of each while looking into the nothingness of each canvas; bespoke Olympias created from scent and imagination.

La toile de lin. A heap of flesh-warmed linens, the sunny breeze of citrus, white flowers and summer herbals—bergamot zest, jasmine, magnolia, lavender, and hyssop. The faintest reminder of her skin's animalic trace on the fabric, musk.

Les bijoux de l'Olympia. The high metallic scent of gold with its slight dullness, the sharp clear one of diamonds, the smooth pearl on its velvet ribbon. Aldehydes and bitter orange peel, honeyed orange blossom alongside the mushroom darkness of indolic gardenia, labdanum and frankincense on moss.

Seulement la peau. The simplicity and complexity of her unadorned skin, its mystery and revelations like shadow and light: overripe peach and persimmon, armfuls of milky-fleshy tuberose, cumin, amber, and benzoin, the earthy mint of fine patchouli.

Les yeux. The depths of her dark eyes, an abyss of woods and spice: cedar and sandalwood, ebony and guiacwood. Smoky-almond tonka bean and creamy carnation. Her pupils, conjured in fiery sparks of clove.

55.

There was never anything of the animal in Olympia. That is, as she is presented, a woman set apart from other women not in reverence but a degradation of womanhood. You say she is 'clearly a venal girl, and more *real* because of it'—what I see is the keeper of a treasury. What else can you do when men persist in coming to you in the guise of a shower of gold? Prudently, you become a banker. The carnal beast, it is us. But I do not hand down that judgement solely to men or wholly disdain them; it is in me as well. Her skin reeks of a cool detachment, the object of lust which has transcended its heated mantle to become an otherworldly being. Even as I stare at her, I smell my own. Too hot as it always has been: perpetually cunt in hand, ripeness in the mouth, both salivating with unknown fruit. A beggar and mother of my own desire.

56.

Page 75, Michel. I remember it because you speak of your prick as a gun, explosive and banal, inextricably tied to the tiresome little death-as-death escape, anxieties and pleasures of the night I have suffered as much as you. But still, *still*, I am not to speak of the centre of my relief—the shock of the old remains the shock of the new. To others, it is an aggression unto itself, without any laughable simile to temper it.

57.

When you were almost eighty and writing about Olympia, I was only six, already captivated by her. What you knew was everything still waiting for me. But had we been able to stand in front of her side by side, we would have shared a breath and with it, a single thought: *it is me she looks at*. Half of it weighted with an adult man's lust and longing, the other half with a child's sensorial ghosts, nameless infatuations unable to define desire beyond a tenderness still unburdened with the complexities of humanity.

58.

Have we not created between us the very thing you wished for, Michel, which is to realise the double trick of writing an imaginary that feels real and a reality wrapped in the haze of dreams; what is Olympia and our double vision of her if not the marriage of these elements? In our transformations—'transfigurations without disfiguration', as you put it—we are invoking the spirit of her. Like the fantasy of Victorine in the mirror, we whisper *Olympia, Olympia*, until the reflection on our pages looks back, entwined with orchids: the man becomes a woman, the woman becomes a dream, the dream transcends us all; this is the alchemy of her painted flesh.

59.

Coming out of the Orsay one late fall afternoon, the last gasp of sun over the Seine is streaked the colour of her hair. It drapes the bridges, tourists frozen in mid-pose or bent sipping hot drinks at café tables, casts its warmth on the cold windows filled with dubious antiquities, masks and totems shivering in a strange land. Even the eternal bouquinistes with their little stands of old volumes cannot escape the tints of her languid sensuality. Like the hair of Edvard Munch's women, it simultaneously possesses and seduces; totality that of a compass rose.

60.

Her orchid reminds me of a calla lily, though they are two completely different flowers. It is the extroverted curls of the petals of one and introverted curl of the petal—for the calla seems to be a single giant one—of the other; one flagrant, the other constrained, a sensual whole. Olympia is likewise both: what the flower exposes the body holds back, even in nudity. Like Robert Mapplethorpe's black and white photos of calla lilies, the formality of their arrangements and monochrome tinting serve to highlight beauty and vulgarity, at the same time mirroring solitude and resolve. Dimitri Levas, Mapplethorpe's former assistant writes, 'Robert was well grounded in the role of flowers in the history of painting. Here the sensual and the prurient are entwined. Robert's flowers are not always about sex, but they are always sensual'. There is solitude in Olympia, not sadness, simply the awareness of purpose and arrangement shared by Mapplethorpe's callas—the intelligence of a particular kind of beauty and its representations.

61.

I see Olympia everywhere, or rather, other Olympias—those also in full possession of who they are, an *Olympianess* which distorts any gaze which seeks to eye and weigh her value like another slab of butcher's flesh hung and displayed. They reign in an uneasy tranquillity: it is us who look upon their majestic serenity with unease, the realisation that the viewer is unnecessary. Above all, the one who is most fitting as consort to Olympia is Francis Bacon's *Portrait of Henrietta Moraes on a Blue Couch*: Olympia self-deformed, more interested in the sexuality of topology, her colours making it appear that she delights in manipulating her softness into the rawness of exposed muscle and sinew. Within the frame, she is a sculpture moulding herself; the ideal form in constant flux. Crucially, she becomes out of reach of desire. Semir Zeki and Tomohiro Ishizu, writing about the neuroesthetics of the artist in *Bacon and the Mind*, note that 'Bacon, though maintaining the relationship between the parts that constitute a body, distorted them severely and added a subversive emotional envelope.' Like the anatomical artwork of skeletons and cadavers by Andreas Vesalius, *Henrietta Moraes* dares, rather than invites, the exploration of what lies beneath—a brutal culling of the passive aesthetic tourist. Wrapping the couch around her, it is no longer a pedestal for display but a fortress. *This body is mine and not yours*, she says. Her own gaze reveals nothing, an opaque, disturbing penetration that mirrors the message of the round door handle. Yellow; once again, warning.

62.

The taste for red, 'the most dazzling colour of all': a colour nowhere in the painting, at least not in the violent purity you speak of. Is it that which you seek in Olympia—in us all—to turn out her pale composed flesh for the heat that her unseen blood promises? Byung-Chul Han says 'the negativity of death is essential to erotic experience'. The car crash sketches you describe, blood-streaked bodies of 'ambient disaster'. From within her boundaries, Olympia looks on impassively: wisdom which comes from the turmoil of our own ichor. The streamlined mundane suddenly exposing the thrill of its destructive possibilities, primal red over contemporary silver, an imaginary emotional landscape of a non-existent Rothko. 'I'm interested only in expressing basic human emotions—tragedy, ecstasy, doom, and so on', said the artist. This is later realised by the artist Paola Pivi in *Camion*, a blood-red overturned truck against silver-grey concrete. Combining Han's sexual 'negativity' and a now-clichéd but still relevant Ballardian sense of industrial frisson with a Bartleby-esque ennui, what is displayed is an uncomfortable blend of pathos, thrill, and indifference, the inevitable existential entrapment of modern life, a deliberately obscured state which Martin Herbert refers to in her works as 'rolling toward but never quite reaching the cognitive shore'. This is not liminality, though it exists in a similar neither-here-nor-there place; it could be better defined as a perpetually incomplete desire, the conscious indecision to choose between the primal and modern, the Limbo of our times. What arises from this chaos becomes the emotional palette of brilliant post-coital colours which paints the erotics of modernity.

63.

Then it struck me, having been unconsciously obsessed with this red with no brutal presence within the frame and which I admit I have projected my own excess upon, I feel an envy of Olympia, who appears the way she does because she is, in a way, rid of men, rid of blood, rid of all the associations which she never asked for: she is not purity nor its opposite, but in taking back the lines of the frame and using them as ones of delineation, she takes back the body as a territory. And I am envious because despite a lifetime of drawing my own maps there is this last battle, with myself; not my head but my blood, which erases my boundary lines time after time until exhausted, I surrender, despising myself for what I see as a weakness I cannot control, as if I believed in the folly of being able to stop and part these sanguine waves as if I were divine. Never having borne anything but failure, Olympia becomes the flesh of my flesh, and I hers. Michel, there is a bittersweet irony in Olympia haunting our shared lacunae, so distant in sex but near in their agonies.

64.

Sometimes the hope of a modernity that will fit us is as simple as the smell of spring rain lingering on pavement. The chromium oxide flowers of Paco Rabanne Metal and Tom Ford Envy: hyacinths, lily of the valley, and musk, the liquid breeze of the unknown over the horizon. Futurism and primalism, heat and cold, the dualism of Olympia. Those perfumes are long discontinued like most futures, but one must also remember the memory of such possibilities go on to create new ones.

65.

I keep moving from your words on writing to those of Duras. My discomfort at coming to 'there always comes a point—if you live long enough—when you no longer feel you belong to your time'. At what place, then, does one write from? You say that it is in fact, death. And I do not disagree, for I know that I have existed there long before I even wrote: not in the sense of the melodramatic—because what is less so than death, the one truism of life—but in a way, I have never existed, feeling so out of place and even being. For me, time meant always running unsuccessfully in an attempt to catch up to somewhere I would be able to exist the way others did. When my father was diagnosed with the illness that would, at least tangentially, lead to his death, he said something on the phone to me. He said only ever expected to live a certain amount of time. This was not mystical, for there was no specific age he had staked this to, like a gambler's favoured number, he simply felt there would be a point in his life where any further expectations on life were akin to an imposition, a guest worried about overstaying his welcome. It struck me as the calmest of statements, a man who sat so comfortably next to death though it had not yet declared it was his time, a man who had spent much of his life by the point I had entered it in solitude, then only in the company of a few people—mostly us, his family—and books. And Duras writes, 'solitude . . . means, either death or a book. But first and foremost it means alcohol.' This, too, struck me with the force of another truth of our family. My father's brother had died of alcoholism, a few years after my father's passing, though unrelated; his spiral came about from a family unable to control its own mythos, though who can, when mired in the belief that it is bestowed? And so I am here, on one hand with much of my father's solitude, the other, the pendulum of my uncle's fate over me. For it has always been there, because it was present in others. My father and I led—lead—our lives as something of a clenched fist; perpetually aware of that siren's song, even in admiration of it, but never quite daring to follow. I find that tightness comes through in writing: a concealed revealing, and not unlike Olympia, I am fully cognisant it must appear to others a frigid attempt at seduction, when in fact it is simply a reluctance to tempt the gods.

66.

Once we are asked to elucidate what we see, it is no longer our own eyes which we look through. The senses are silent and solitary, preferring to radiate their invisible knowledge like hyphal networks in search of their kin.

67.

Distantly, parts of a story I read when I was young keep entering my thoughts, a macabre tale of a beautiful woman who constantly wore a black ribbon round her throat. I am recalling it—perhaps incorrectly, though I think there is still truth in misremembered things, the mind adjusting to what fits one's circumstances—as her lover pleaded with her to remove it, until the pleading became torment and the ribbon was removed, by her hand or his, I no longer know, and her head fell off. I go back and forth from this to the idea when women write, they are also wearing that ribbon, plagued by others' determination to discover whatever it is they are so insistent is being hidden from them. The irony is, *it* is nothing; we are just a scattering of pieces we do our best to keep together.

68.

Solitary practices such as writing separate lovers of instruments from lovers of noise. Without an audience, we must place the utmost trust in our inner ear in order to discern truth from self-flattery.

I do not know if I trust my own silence, Michel. Is the truth I am trying to draw out of use to anyone, not least of all, myself? The truth is that the truth is useless; if I think of those playing cards from so long ago, what I see I try to connect, but what I connect others cannot see or would connect to something else I cannot see. I am describing a world that may only exist to myself—as you say, 'a mesmerizing tour of the contents of your brain', which is difficult to read without hearing more than just a touch of sarcasm in it—will it affect anything or just fall flat as an affectation? You say trying to explain the how or writing then crashes into why which inevitably leaves us in the midst of endless doubts as to why we decided to embark on this rather foolish and overly-travelled journey to begin with. I think we both know we are naked and remain so, and it is not a case of exhibitionism as much as the fetish of examination, to examine and be examined: a good patient but better study—here is the one they will write about! Coming from a family where my grandfather was a doctor, it is hard not to view everything I do at times as an examination. I am a doctor, my subjects are patients, more often than not I am my own subject, which seems to be a conflict of interest, but also explains my attempts at detachment in writing. Whereas there are moments where I wonder, would this tour of my brain be more effective were I hysterical instead of studied, mimicked symptoms to prolong the attention instead of behave as I always have, quiet on the chair or table, only a faint wheeze or issue invisible to anything but biopsies or scans like a trail to be followed only by the dedicated. And then I take up my instruments again: *breathe in, breathe out*, listening for whatever it is that wishes to make itself known.

69.

I have to come back to her hands. Despite the controversy of Olympia, what I find most fascinating lies there, in how she positions them: all I see are the hands of Gertrude Stein. (Here is that 'utilitarian utility' you feel is absent, Michel, rapt in the image of Olympia as seduction. It seems the 'sorcerer's hands' which created her were not strong enough to glaze her solely in fantasy; this is the 'fine detail' of a personality unquelled). Immovable, as if they contained their own personalities—and they do, for as Rilke, writing about the sculptures of Rodin, says, 'hands have a history . . . their own wishes, feelings, moods . . .'. The set of the hand mirrors the set of the mouth. Now I look again, and see everything is set. The jaws are set, clenched with an almost-invisible tension—the anticipation of critique, of comment. The eyes are set, looking out but never allowing ingress. No, the observer must find more amenable entries into these personas. The noses do not twitch or wrinkle. All judgements slide off their straightness, given no purchase. The hands are set and still. The hands are thinking. The hands are thinking of others looking at their hands, for we look at hands when the face gives nothing away. What the faces do not give away the hands follow in example. This is my face, these are my hands, we are immovable.

70.

There are days where I feel like Giacometti's sculpture of an arm, my dissociation so extreme nothing is left but a limb writing people and experiences I no longer remember.

71.

I remember what John Berger said in an essay about Giacometti, his death resulted in a kind of distillation in his creations, the essence of 'being seen'. In the case of the fully formed bodies, 'if you stare, the figure stares back'. But with the fragments—the arms, noses, legs, appendages suspended in and out of time—they are 'observers of his future absence, his death, his becoming unknowable.' So what are these fragments I am writing, Michel? Unable to see the essence of myself in my physical body, I turn to Olympia's to see and be seen. These slivers and splinters from a textual body are presented for examination, both post-mortem and vivisection: the opening and closing of one's eyes in order to understand the presence and absence of self simultaneously. I see the disconnected limbs, but it is I who is the phantom.

72.

My father gave me necklaces: a rose gold, flower-adorned locket, empty; a silver chain with a handmade ivory and silver axe; a gold chain set with an oval green tourmaline; gold chain with a gold shell pendant; book-shaped enamel locket, empty.

The sacraments my father placed round my neck, the high holiness of the meaning of objects. Lost to the carelessness of time loss becomes realisation. Disguised in metals and jewels, he gave me my future self; not an attempt at creation but a trail of clues signifying what I would become. As e. e. cummings says:

> (now the ears of my ears awake and
> now the eyes of my eyes are opened)

What is this but an attempt of a collector to replicate in words the meanings of objects never explained, to pin down the delicate lessons that flew about her, unawares, as a child? But I cannot give them that life, no matter how light or dreamlike I place them on their pages. That life is gone, as all collectors secretly know: chasing memories whose wings can no longer be felt in gossamer motion, our ungraceful fingers mimicking their distant flights against the nets of our skin.

73.

A handful of primal figures strung on cords, charmless charms which rose and fell with his last breath. I cannot bear to place that tangle of leather and stone round my own neck, knowing they hold a specific heat and cold, the passing from one place to another. I have wondered what magic it was he hoped to possess, remembering he always wore a necklace of some sort. Fancies of his imagination took the form of corals or carvings often made by his own hand, tokens of lives unlived as he spent his days the image of the man he was expected to be, creating the future. The necklace as validation of what remained unexposed: within his setting of angles and metal, what happens when modernity is unable to imagine a future already present, the clash of languor and speed which denies the realisation of dreams? My father, trapped somewhere between Olympia and Tamara de Lempicka's *Autoportrait*, holding on to the man he wished to be.

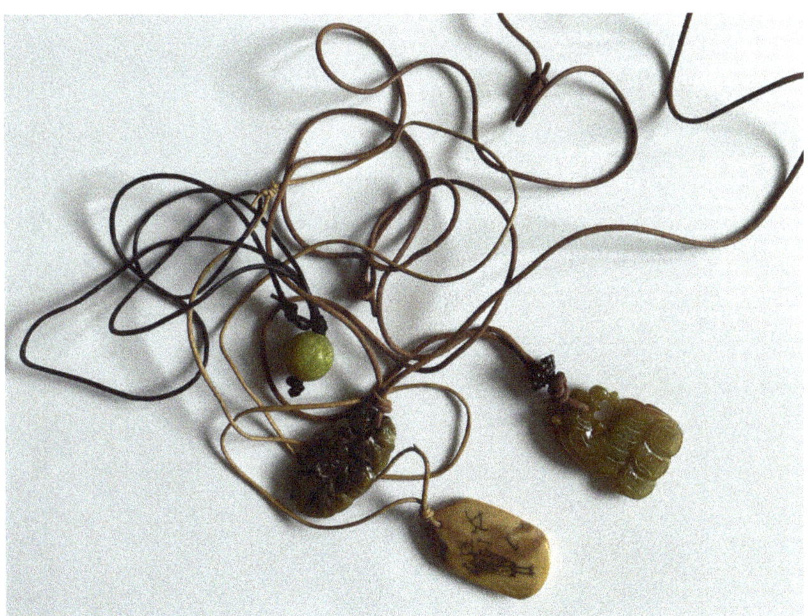

74.

Who would Victorine have painted had she produced a self-portrait: side by side, would one be unrecognisable from the other, twin strangers exchanging stories of familiar but separate lives? *I* plus *I* equals distance; any recognition of Victorine as Olympia means the former's existence creates a suspicion of belief in the viewer. What one sees, one believes, until one sees what one cannot believe. If she were to carefully cut away Olympia's form from the canvas, who would the viewer fill that space with which would continue to fulfil its meaning? Or would she, clever woman, have placed her cutout next to herself, both in front of that now incomplete frame, inviting others to view Olympia, Victorine, and the void as a woman of multitudes and a multitude of women?

75.

The red of Leiris to the blue of William Gass. From Olympia to his (Gass's) neighbour's wife, 'that buxom wench with the inviting eyes . . . innocent and unaware, preparing salad at the sink'. A template for voyeurism which shifts through the years yet stays the same. The ideal copy as a design for desire. It is the wise man who recognizes that women are Heraclitus's river; never identical, yet all able to drown those who dismiss her. Woman avenges in colour: the warning yellow of Henri Regnault's *Salome*, the demon-temptresses of Domenico Morelli's *Le tentazioni di Sant'Antonio*, half-hidden in rush mats—laughing, only partially exposing themselves in glimpses of nipples and red lips in the knowledge that what is not seen invites further madness, Helle Contou's *Jezebel*, resplendent and streaked warlike in yellow, red, blue, and black, pose recalling Hans Holbein the Younger's *Anne of Cleves*. Olympia's muted tones seem not unlike

Gass's fantasy, but all the while, Zola's words in *Au Bonheur des Dames* murmur, 'there will be one who'll have revenge for them all'.

76.

Michel, I know there are those who would dismiss you and others on the basis of a single thought or passage, reading into it a universe of offense. Whether those lines had sprung lightly, instinctually, or had been considered with a philosophical weight and gravity, does it make any difference? Take the previous part: who would I be if said about Gass, this single fantasy is unbearable, so therefore the man must be the same, and henceforth condemn all future writings? I have had the same fantasies: the fleetest of things emerging from a fragment of lust, which as featherweight as it is, occupies a place of seriousness because it is undeniably part of me. Lust occupies no place of moral purity, nor in its opposite. But its simplicity is forever damned as complexity, for the one who lusts can never truly convey the clarity of the feeling unless both are connected with that rare electricity; to explain the process negates the charge. I think, traitorous as it may seem, such lines—his and your own—are celebratory. If I appear to clash with them, I still celebrate them for being honest, for it is only in the conflict of such honesty I may approach my own.

77.

It is easy to guess what her scent could be, but impossible to know what it was. Back then? Verbena, rose, violet, lily, opopanax, amber, patchouli, real musk. She *appears* scentless, curiously stripped in another way, though the ghost of the most intimate flesh reminds us, *never completely*. Laure, posing as the maid, takes on those tangible glories, arms abundant with blossom; a Black Flora in a White house.

Olympia, clean but secretly dirty. As Hélène Cixous says, *propre*, as explained by Betsy Wing, her translator:

> It [propre] also means 'proper', 'appropriate', and 'clean' . . . since woman must care for bodily needs and instill the cultural values of cleanliness and propriety, she is deeply involved in what is propre, yet she is always somehow suspect, never quite propre herself.

An olfactory blank slate which can be erased and redrawn to the order and demands of pleasure, but more than that, acceptability.

78.

So many flowers, though orchids and lilies seems to predominate when it comes to Olympia: the sacred and the profane. I am still considering her smell—I *need* to know the smell of her. An impossible completion, I realise, but it is the same way when one finally smells a lover's skin and understands how they match your own. It is unthinkable that in trying to breathe into her a life which would allow her to step out of the frame, I would forget to bestow her with scent—to garland her in them like that glorious jewelled breast. Olympia has not received but deserves the treatment which *Lá Venus de Milo* and *Lá Victoire de Samothrace* have at the hands of perfumer-apothecary Buly 1803; cool marbles wreathed in heat: the former with heliotrope, jasmine, amber, and musk, the latter with tuberose, magnolia, jasmine, and myrrh. Looking at my own collection with its different facets of desires and possibilities, what a true revealing it would be to paint her surrounded with her own bottles: the scent of self, a Song of Songs sung only to and for herself. What play there is within each flacon! Will Olympia adorn herself in Etat Libre d'Orange Secretions Magnifiques, with its salty-floral, deliberately post-coital scent, every bit the framed fantasy? Or will it be their Dangerous Complicity, with its laughing sting of ginger and rum, flesh-ripe fruits and musky-dark corners hinting at her taste for anyone and everyone who takes her fancy? Perhaps she will reject everything in her seen identity of skin and heat, and anoint herself instead with Comme des Garçons Concrete, the cold clean scent of a new world whose machined blossoms have barely started to bud. But I return to Leonard Cohen's scented oil, which reminds me that Olympia's body above all holds a reverence beyond flesh and earth. A plume of memory rises in my nostrils, of a bottle once owned that smelled of lilies and incense both cool and warm: like Mapplethorpe's callas, the essence of sexuality and sensuality seen through a lens that gives it a different kind of bloom. L'Artisan Parfumeur's Passage d'Enfer; how fitting it is for such beauty to go through hell before it finds its calm, but remembering the words of Louise Bourgeois's 1996 work *Untitled (I Have Been to Hell and Back)*:

> And Let Me
> Tell You,
> It Was
> Wonderful.

79.

The ribbon as 'the final obstacle to total nudity', as if we were necessarily something to be completed along the lines of an assault course or a battlefield laid with traps. Michel, I find these linguistic hostilities so casually strewn about the text somehow natural to the state of woman. Natural in that we do not view your bodies as a war to be won, but in knowing this is how you view us, one must at least defend one's territory. Yet for all this I see the poor affection in it, a boy playing at soldiers so that he may win the devotion of his playmates.

80.

The new problem is no one looks for the old joy of it. The previous formality of direct sight which was paid her is now obsolete; removed, transferred from painting to the self through a myriad of other eyes and frames. A screen, a face, her image. The one held in between now observed by both active and passive audiences, neither with the option to refuse. A two-way frame which demands and ensures constant viewing, what had been a tendril of an oligopticon becomes the panopticon, a surveillance entertainment where the only fear is one of no longer being seen. What had once been the flâneur of the museum becomes the badaud: fascinated only by shining new reflections, their face in every work of art. But in this modern gaze, a freedom. Olympia is released to view the world as its rightful flâneuse; no longer subject or object, an observer.

81.

I am drawn to the strange depth in her left eye. The dot of light in it a bored (in both senses) hole letting out what? Impatience? Amusement? Knowing? Rage? Maybe the great irony is, what she is immortalised for in the painting was in that situation, free labour. Pascal Quignard says, 'we unwittingly become the image we shall never know'. Victorine/Olympia knew, complicit in her own transformation. Collaborating with her body to create a woman destined to be scrutinised for what she wasn't but *could* be, in the way all women must be chameleons of circumstance. For the body is an intrigue, and if we are conspirators, it is because it is the only way to retain some semblance of possession over it, and as such, its survival. Her eye looks past the horizon not with what you call 'indifference', but infinite wisdom at the immediate audience to come, ones to follow. Years and decades and centuries pass; what lingers is the gaze which she continues to hope can look beyond, not merely at her. It is us who have always mistaken her, Michel, and in doing so, ourselves.

82.

Now more than ever, she would twist her arm to look at the pale underside of skin untouched by the sun, look twice in the mirror at a face experience stripped of vanity with a studied curiosity reminiscent of how she would look at the chessboard or the nuances of her tint in the midst of another great loss of red. Though she was not touched by it again, she began to welcome the feeling that syncope was never far away, the lucid companion of certain illnesses which shed its light of reflective wisdom on women. She lay on the bed, looking up at lights through half-shut eyes, the dancing shapes of an event horizon or magnifying what she saw beneath her lids like bacteria in gilded petri dishes. She held up her arms, finely networked with veins, and imagined them as turned cards: *The Tower of Olympia, The Yellow Light, The Fire-Eater, Blood, The Void, The Calla Lily, The Lady of the Perfumes*. Laid out on the bed, her body was a reading. Skin is never wholly smooth or monochrome, something she learned rubbing sheets of in her mother's roughly silken Japanese calligraphy pads between her fingers as a child, the random arrangements of its strands a language not yet known to her. Later she would read Junichirō Tanizaki writing about washi, how it absorbed light and soothed the senses in a way Western paper did not, and understood her kinship with Olympia's familiar shades, the unflushed glow which reminded her of a lamp veiled by the gauze of a curtain, a woman displayed but unrevealed. What she had lost in red she gained in light; the divine incandescence of Olympia.

NOTES

vii ***The Ribbon at Olympia's Throat***: Leiris, Michel. *The Ribbon at Olympia's Throat*, trans. Christine Pichini (South Pasadena, California: Semiotext(e), 2019) [*RIB*]

vii **expressive power of fetishism . . . labyrinthine expressive power of fetishism**: Davis, Lydia. *Essays One* (New York: Picador, 2019,) 392.

1 **Unable to tattoo everything**: *RIB*, 15.

2 **there are paintings which are excited**: Roland Barthes, "The Wisdom of Art," in *Writings on Twombly*, ed. Nicola Del Roscio (Munich: Schirmer/Mosel Publishers, 2002) [*WOA*], 113.

2 **reversing the usual relationship in classical technique**: Roland Barthes, *WOA*, 113.

3 **I'm speaking in order to speak**: *RIB*, 10.

3 **I am on the edge of that madness**: *RIB*, 110.

4 **I want to say**: *RIB*, 10.

4 **I only speak**: *RIB*, 11.

4 **expend so many words**: *RIB*, 64.

6 **Or other fragment of a body**: *RIB*, 27.

7 **a production of Verdi's *Macbeth***: Teatro Regio of Turin's production of Verdi's *Macbeth*, directed by Emma Dante and conducted by Gianandrea Noseda at the 2017 Edinburgh International Festival.

7 **it's as if plants were growing**: *RIB*, 112.

8 **a 1984 advertisement**: I collect vintage magazine advertisements. This one is attributed to Boucheron jewellers, Paris, thought to be from 1984. Photographer unknown.

9 **COURTESAN REALITIES STOP**: *RIB*, 218.

9 **he was waiting, too**: Maupassant, Guy de. *Bel-Ami*, trans. Douglas Parmée (London: Penguin Books Ltd, 1975), 27.

12 **The detail we touch**: *RIB*, 17.

13 **Modernity, eternity**: *RIB*, 7.

16 ***eternity*** **. . . gives the resounding sensation**: *RIB*, 229.

16 **the thing that's between us**: Duras, Marguerite. *Practicalities*, trans. Barbara Bray (New York: Grove Press, 1990) [*PRA*], 39.

17 **regret when I do bad work**: *RIB*, 115.

18 **You cannot know both hands at once**: Stewart, Susan. *Columbarium* (Chicago and London: The University of Chicago Press, 2005), 42.

18 **who knows too well**: *RIB*, 257.

20 **while Lipton felt assimilated**: Brown, Elspeth H. *Work! The Queer History of Modeling* (Durham and London: Duke University Press, 2019), 240.

25 **a dream of protection**: Bachelard, Gaston. *The Poetics of Space*, trans. Maria Jolas (Boston: Beacon Press, 1994) [*POS*], 101.

25 **Dreams of a garment-house**: Bachelard, Gaston. *POS*, 101.

25 **ruin refers to a fabric**: Stewart, Susan. *The Ruins Lesson: Meaning and Material in Western Culture* (Chicago and London: The University of Chicago Press, 2020), 1.

26 **a caress**: Derrida, Jacques. *On Touching—Jean Luc Nancy*, trans. Christine Irizarry (Stanford, California: Stanford University Press, 2005), 93.

27 **our daily life**: Bergson, Henri. *Matter and Memory*, trans. N.M. Paul and W.S. Palmer (New York: Zone Books, 1991), 95.

28 **text without end**: Barthes, Roland. *The Language of Fashion*, trans. Andy Stafford (London and New York: Bloomsbury, 2013), 26.

29 **a uniform**: Duras, Marguerite. *PRA*, 65.

30 **Rilke imagines us angry**: Gross, Kenneth. *The Dream of the Moving Statue* (University Park, Pennsylvania: The Pennsylvania State University Press, 2006), 155.

30 **grief felt for the person who has died**: Strawson, Galen. *Things That Bother Me* (New York: New York Review Books, 2018), 85.

31 **death, the fact of death coming towards you**: Duras, Marguerite. *PRA*, 64.

32 **we don't forget**: Barthes, Roland. *Mourning Diary*, trans. Richard Howard (London: Notting Hill Editions, 2011), 227

34 **It is no new thing**: Beauvoir, Simone de. *Brigitte Bardot and the Lolita Syndrome*, trans. Bernard Fretchman (London: Four Square Books, 1962) [*BBL*], 6.

34 **They are obliged to recognize**: Beauvoir, Simone de. *BBL*, 34.

34 **She offers herself directly**: Beauvoir, Simone de. *BBL*, 46.

34 **The debunking of love and eroticism**: Beauvoir, Simone de. *BBL*, 58.

35 **the creature**: *RIB*, 70.

35 **Ah, ah**: Hoffmann, E.T.A. *Tales of Hoffmann*, trans. R.J. Hollingdale, Stella and Vernon Humphries, Sally Hayward (London: Penguin Books, 1982), 115.

35 **an ornament with no soul**: *RIB*, 70.

37 **my way of existing**: *RIB*, 158.

39 **disorder is surrender**: Leduc, Violette. *Mad in Pursuit*, trans. Derek Coltman (London: Panther Books, 1972), 82.

39 **There is no ideal body**: Wangenheim, Chris von. In *Fashion: Theory*, ed. Carol di Grappa (New York: Lustrum Press, 1980), 155.

39 **porno**: *RIB*, 61.

40 **Gia and I would go out**: Gross, Michael. *Model: The Ugly Business of Beautiful Women* (New York: It Books, 2011), 348.

40 **the intimate muff concealed**: *RIB*, 151.

41 **enribbon . . . enseminate** : *RIB*, 145.

42 **a 1971 photograph**: Lutens, Serge. *Berlin à Paris* (Milano: Mondadori Electa, 2012), 22–23

44 **the trauma is a product of its repetition**: Stewart, Susan. *Crimes of Writing* (Oxford and New York: Oxford University Press, 1991) [*COW*], 278.

44 **we should remember that the very first defining trait**: Stewart, Susan. *COW*, 281.

46 **the past in ruins**: *RIB*, 248.

46 **discordant ear**: *RIB*, 248.

46 **the past, pierced by so many memory holes**: *RIB*, 248.

46 **scents . . . are able to stabilize a self**: Han, Byung-Chul. *The Scent of Time*, trans. Daniel Steuer (Cambridge and Medford, Massachusetts: Polity Press, 2017), 45–46.

47 **'trying to find some charm in its perfume**: *RIB*, 226.

47 **obsession is important in art**: Lutens, Serge. *L'esprit Serge Lutens: The Spirit of Beauty* (Paris: Assouline 1992) [*ESL*], 187.

47 **to look at a picture**: Lutens, Serge. *ESL*, 187.

48 **the *I Magma* app**: The two images and corresponding text in this section were generated by the *I Magma* app (i-magma.ai) which had been given an image of Manet's *Olympia*.

54 **Louise Bourgeois's *Sainte Sébastienne***: 'Louise Bourgeois: An Unfolding Portrait', MoMA online.

56 **a wandering stroll taken by thought**: *RIB*, 170.

57 **What do you think you're looking at?**: *RIB*, 38.

57 **Her scent escapes**: Huysmans, J.-K. *Parisian Sketches*, trans. Brendan King (Cambridge: Dedalus European Classics, 2014), 127.

58 **intimate resonance**: *RIB*, 179.

58 **glow / pulsate / odorize** : *RIB*, 180.

58 **what do you do when everything is available**: Baudrillard, Jean. *America*, trans. Chris Turner (London and New York: Verso Books, 2010), 30.

59 **rose and floral folds**: *RIB*, 151.

60 **black is the sign of the offering**: Badiou, Alain. *Black: The Brilliance of a Non-Color*, trans. Susan Spitzer (Cambridge and Malden: Polity Books, 2019), 63.

60 **There's an abyssal bliss**: Herbert, Martin. *The Uncertainty Principle* (Berlin: Sternberg Press, 2014) [*UNC*], 106.

61 **The senses are asked to process simultaneously**: Herbert, Martin. *UNC*, 102–103.

61 **what is truth?**: Wharton, Edith. *The House of Mirth* (Ware: Wordsworth Editions, 2002), 197.

62 **clearly a venal girl**: *RIB*, 70.

63 **your prick as a gun**: *RIB*, 75.

63 **transfigurations without disfiguration**: *RIB*, 171.

64 **Robert was well grounded in the role of flowers**: 'From Book to Bid—Mapplethorpe's Calla Lily', www.phaidon.com.

65 **Bacon, though maintaining the relationship**: Zeki, Semir and Ishizu, Tomohiro. 'The "Visual Shock" of Francis Bacon: An Essay in Neuroesthenics' in *Bacon and the Mind: Art, Neuroscience and Psychology* (Francis Bacon Studies 1), ed. Martin Harrison (London: Thames & Hudson, 2019), 127.

66 **the most dazzling colour of all**: *RIB*, 43.

66 **the negativity of death**: Han, Byung-Chul. *The Agony of Eros*, trans. Erik Butler (Cambridge and London: The MIT Press, 2017), 24.

66 **ambient disaster**: *RIB*, 43.

66 **rolling toward but never quite reaching the cognitive shore**: Herbert, Martin. *UNC*, 104.

67 **there always comes a point**: *RIB*, 219.

68 **solitude . . . means**: Duras, Marguerite. *Writing*, trans. Mark Polizzotti (Minneapolis: The University of Minnesota Press, 2011), 7.

70 **a mesmerizing tour of the contents of your brain**: *RIB*, 174.

70 **utilitarian utility**: *RIB*, 46.

71 **sorcerer's hands**: *RIB*, 46.

71 **fine detail**: *RIB*, 46.

71 **hands have a history**: Rilke, Rainer Maria. *Rodin and Other Prose Pieces*, trans. G. Craig Houston (London: Quartet Books, 1986), 19.

71 **being seen . . . if you stare back . . . observers of his future absence** : Berger, John. *About Looking*. (London: Bloomsbury Books, 2009), 183.

72 **My father gave me necklaces**: A reference to Leiris's line, 'My father gave me rubies'. *RIB*, 18.

72 **now the ears of my ears awake** : cummings e.e. *Selected Poems* (London: Faber and Faber, 1997), 92.

74 **that buxom wench with the inviting eyes**: Gass, William. *On Being Blue* (New York: New York Review Books, 2014) 79.

75 **there will be one who'll have revenge for them all**: Zola, Émile. *The Ladies' Paradise*, trans. Robin Buss (London: Penguin Books, 2001), 68, Apple Books.

76 **It also means 'proper'** : Cixous Hélène and Clément, Catherine. *The Newly Born Woman*, trans. Betsy Wing (Minneapolis and Oxford: University of Minneapolis Press, 1991), 167.

77 **And Let Me Tell You** : *Untitled (I Have Been To Hell and Back)*. Louise Bourgeois, www.artsy.net.

77 **the final obstacle to total nudity**: *RIB*, 194.

78 **we unwittingly become the image we shall never know**: Quignard, Pascal. *The Sexual Night*, trans. Chris Turner (London; New York; Calcutta: Seagull Books, 2014), 105.

78 **indifference**: *RIB*, 209.

79 **washi**: Tanizaki, Junichirō. *In Praise of Shadows*, trans. Thomas J. Harper and Edward G. Seidensticker (London: Vintage Books, 2001), 17.

Acknowledgements

This book would not exist if it were not for Michel Leiris, but even more so, the passion of Semiotext(e) and the translator Christine Pichini in bringing him to an English-language audience. I am forever thankful for the time and labour of all the publishers and translators that make it possible for me to access such writers.

I am full of gratitude to Jacob Smullyan at Sagging Meniscus and Guillermo Stitch at *Exacting Clam* for the simplicity of trust. That is the essence of what it means to write—the words are enough, if you are given the freedom to do with them as you wish.

Part of chapter 25 was originally published as 'Metamorphosis' online in *Vestoj*. My thanks to Anja Aronowsky Cronberg.

There would be no me as I now know her without the two Js. What I owe them is the one thing I cannot articulate.

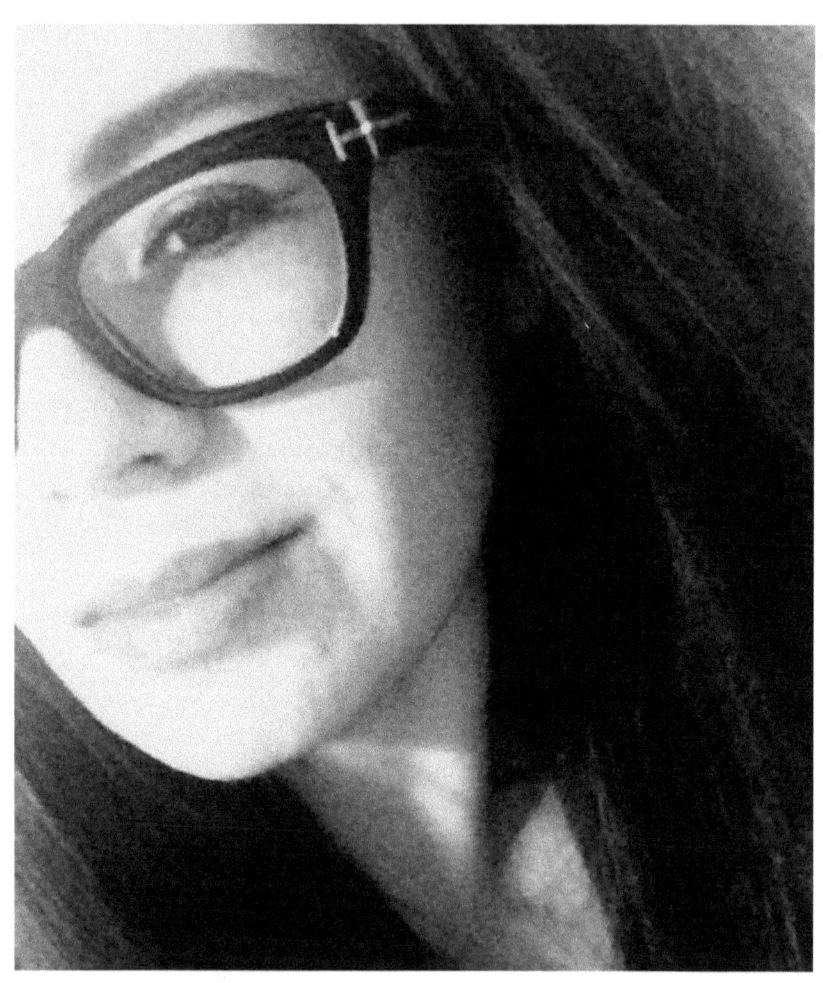

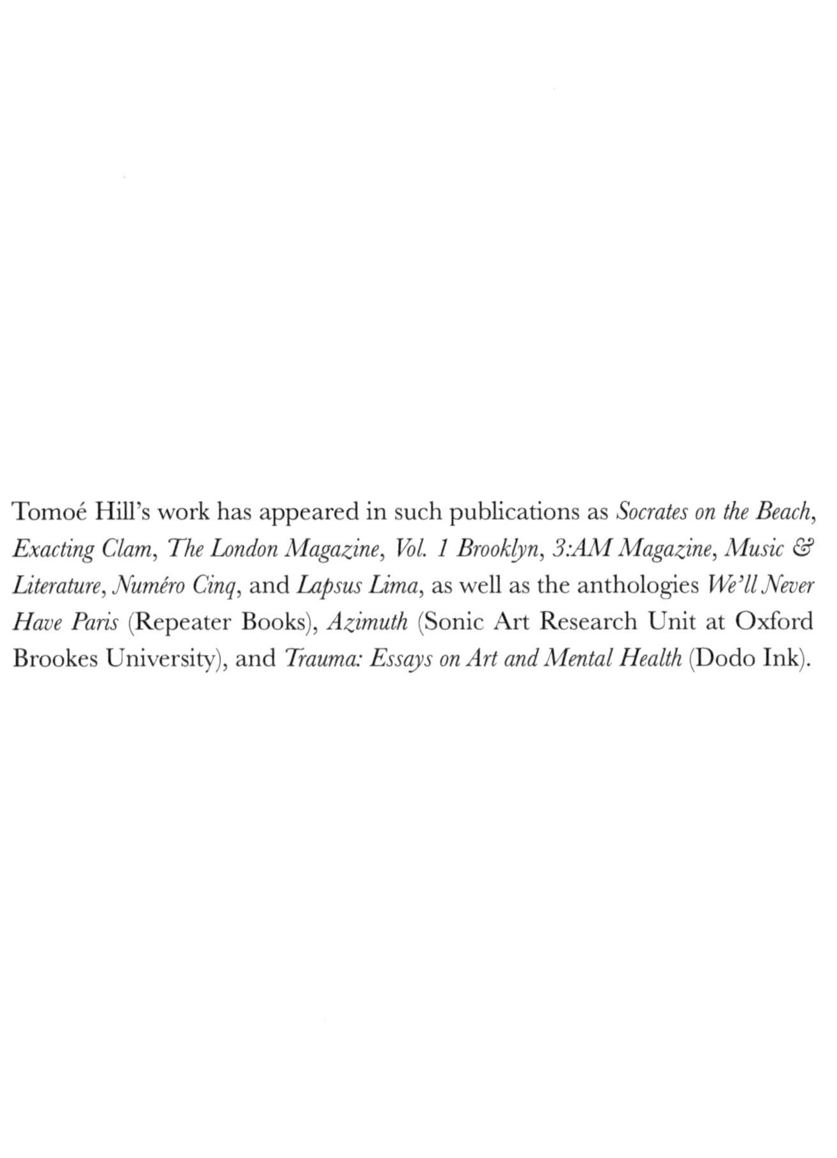

Tomoé Hill's work has appeared in such publications as *Socrates on the Beach*, *Exacting Clam*, *The London Magazine*, *Vol. 1 Brooklyn*, *3:AM Magazine*, *Music & Literature*, *Numéro Cinq*, and *Lapsus Lima*, as well as the anthologies *We'll Never Have Paris* (Repeater Books), *Azimuth* (Sonic Art Research Unit at Oxford Brookes University), and *Trauma: Essays on Art and Mental Health* (Dodo Ink).

www.ingramcontent.com/pod-product-compliance
Lightning Source LLC
LaVergne TN
LVHW052355100826
845147LV00013B/846
* 9 7 8 1 9 5 2 3 8 6 6 7 1 *